AF673172

Rajasthan

Colours of a Desert Land

Rajasthan

Dr. Surendra Sahai

Published by Brijbasi Art Press Ltd.
E 46/11 Okhla Industrial Area, Phase II
New Delhi 110020
E-mail: brijbasi@bol.net.in
Website: www.brijbasiartpress.com

Text by Surendra Sahai
Designed by: Yogesh Suraksha Design Studio
www.ysdesignstudio.com

ISBN 81-87902-05-1

Processed at Brijbasi Art Press Ltd.
Printed and bound in Singapore

Photocredits:
Aditya Patankar: page 4-5,18-19, 22-23, 24-25, 26-27, 28-29, 34-35, 36-37, 40, 98-99; Amit Pasricha: 16-17, 67, 85, 127, 146, 166,168; Avinash Pasricha: 108-109, Gopi Gajwani 38, 80-81, 89, 128-129, 147; P.K. De: 2-3, 70-71, 74,184-185; Prakash Israni: 41(top), 48, 64,163; Rajbir Singh courtesy National museum, New Delhi: 172-173, 174, 177, 181, 190-191; Rajesh Bedi: Cover, 6, 10-11, 14-15, 39, 41(bottom), 42-43, 44-45, 88, 90-91, 96-97, 120, 150-151; Rajpal Singh: 1, 76-77, 118, 121, 179(top); Gen R.K.Gaur: 52-53, 141,148, 158-159, 188-189; Rupinder Khullar: 46-47, 51, 56-57, 86, 100-101,102-103, 106 (bottom), 119, 143, 152-153, 192; Shalini Saran: 30, 31, 32, 33, 66, 82-83, 84, 87, 94, 116-117, 139; Shivji: 12-13, 60-61; Subhash Bhargava :20, 62, 92,106 (top),110-111, 122-123, 126, 130-131, 134, 144-145, 154, 160-161, 162, 164 (top), 169, 170-171, 179 (bottom), 186,187; Sudhir Kasliwal: 8-9, 72-73, 93, 95, 164 (bottom), 165; Suraj Sharma: 113; Surendra Sahai: 58-59, 114-115, 124-125, 156-157; Tarun Chopra: 55, 63, 65, 68-69, 132-133, 136-137, 149

Contents

Introduction

The present book is not a history of Rajasthan. It is only a modest attempt at introducing the reader to the glorious cultural and architectural heritage of this splendid state of India. Rajasthan is a large state divided by the Aravalli Ranges, believed to be geologically the world's oldest fold mountains. On the east lies the green, fertile and forest area watered by rivers and lakes. On the west lies the Thar desert guarded on the borders by the forts at Jaisalmer and Bikaner. Rajasthan has undergone tremendous cataclysmic geological shifts. The Thar is a reminder of a time, millions and millions years ago, when the land lay covered by the sea.

The Rajputs, legendary warriors appeared on the scene in the medieval period and, though small in number, carved out small but strong kingdoms for themselves on the sandy and hilly regions. They created a distinctive romantic aura about their class by their unflinching adherence to a code of honour, valour and chivalry. Their fiercest battles were fought with the Delhi Sultans and the Mughal emperors.

The forts and palaces in Rajasthan are examples of the most spectacular architecture of dynastic power and strategic military defences created by the proud rulers. They symbolise for modern visitors the grandeur and opulence of the Rajput courts, their legendary wealth, their turbulent history and their readiness to fight and embrace death, if defeated. In the dark labyrinthine underground passages in many a fort, you might see

"in the midst 'mong thousand heraldries,
And twilight saints, and dim emblazonings,
A shielded escutcheon blush'd with
Blood of queens and kings" (John Keats)

The vast majority of people in Rajasthan lead a life of struggle against the rigours of a harsh, dry and hot climate. But they are ever smiling and cheerful, celebrating every occasion with music and dance. Their arts and crafts reflect the grandeur of vibrant colour. Their dress has the widest range of stunning colours-bright red, yellow, green, blue, shocking pink, white and black. Even a single woman clad in her usual skirt, blouse and odhni looks a carnival of dazzling hues. Men, usually dressed in a white dhoti and shirt, wear turbans in most glorious colours. The vast congregations of village folk drawn from far-flung villages to the seasonal fairs, as at Pushkar, create a veritable sea of humanity clad in the most dazzling peacock colours, shattering the drabness of the bleak sandscape.

This is Rajasthan, land of ancient origin, home of the valiant Rajputs and the most charming and colourful people.

The Magnificent Rajputs

Rajput palaces all over the state contain a great number of wall paintings that depict warriors in typical Rajasthani costume; note the flower in the left hand and the sword in the right hand. *Preceding page:* Maharaja Gaj Singh of Jodhpur sits in *darbar* at the most colourful and ornamental Takht Mahal in the Fort of Jodhpur.

History has portrayed the Rajputs as brave warriors, streaming out of their strongholds, swords gleaming in the sun, facing death with a defiant pride. The Rajputs carved out kingdoms in the harsh desert and built magnificent forts and palaces. They were the last of the fabulous breed of adventurous kings. Their valour and exploits is the stuff legends are made of and inspired the balladeers of the desert, who, to this day, sing their praises. The Rajputs belonged, to the *kshatriya* or warrior caste. They emerged in Rajasthan in the sixth and seventh centuries as the royal clans of the Pratiharas, Solankis, Paramars, Guhilas, Chauhans, and Kachhwahas. They dominated the history of the region till the end of the medieval era.

The origin of the Rajputs remains shrouded in the realms of myth and legend. The historian, Harbans Mukhia, writes about the heated controversy which has raged over this subject: "National pride no doubt played a part in influencing the insistence of those favouring Indian origin. However, more recently, the general consensus is that Rajput clans owe their birthright to both indigenous and foreign origins." Given the rigid social structure of those times, the upward mobility of castes was practically impossible. So, the indigenous warriors and foreign invaders, who had established their own kingdoms resolved the problem, by the virtue of a ritual purification by fire. This enabled them to reassert their status as warriors and to declare themselves as *rajaputras*, the sons of kings. To, further reinforce this newly-found glory, they were assigned descent from the sun and the moon. Family trees listed epic heroes of the calibre of Lord Rama of Ayodhya and Lord Krishna of Dwarka. Thus emerged the clans of Suryavanshi or descendants of the sun and Chandravanshi or descendants of the moon. Ritually purified descendants of foreign invading tribes, such as the Huns, too, were given "caste status" as warriors. Thus, Rajputs originating from various regions and classes formed a homogenous social caste embracing a strict code of honour, which became integral to their character.

The most illustrious of the Rajputs, the Chauhans, were destined to play a crucial role in resisting Muslim invasions from across the north-western frontiers. They ruled the area around Ajmer, and began as feudatories of the Pratiharas. Prithviraj Chauhan III, the bravest among them was king of Delhi when Mohammed Ghori invaded the city in 1191. The battle at Tarain was won by Prithviraj, who, in an act of habitual chivalry, freed Ghori. It was the kind of noble graciousness only a Rajput could extend. Sadly, Ghori returned and the brave Prithviraj fell to the hands of the astute and cunning invader. After his earlier, well-earned victory over

Ghori he had made no allowance for his enemy's unexpected return. He was completely unprepared for this tactical stroke of genius on the part of Ghori. Defeated and killed in battle, Prithviraj Chauhan lost the only chance the Rajputs had of establishing a Hindu rule over north India. Rajasthani bards sing in praise of Prithviraj's unbridled bravery and of his romantic elopement with Princess Sanyukta, the daughter of King Jaichand of Kannauj. He rode off with her, in the course of a *swayamvara*, a ceremony in which a princess chooses her husband.

The Guhilots of Mewar rose to power in the tenth century. Their first chieftain was born in a cave, so they came to be called Guhilot, which means "cave born". The history of Mewar is written in blood; it is one of tragic sacrifice, suicidal courage, and loyal valour. Mewar faced three invasions which led to massacres and the ritual of *jauhar* by proud women, who preferred death by fire rather than dishonour as captives. There is the enduring legend, of Queen Padmini and Alauddin Khalji, the Sultan of Delhi. He besieged Chittor and offered to withdraw, only if he could have a glimpse of the queen. It is said, he was allowed a fleeting glimpse of the legendary beauty in a mirror as she stood on the steps of her lake pavilion. Padmini's husband, Rana Ratan Singh, escorted Alauddin out of the fort, but the traitorous Sultan seized the Rajput king at the last gate. The message, sent to the queen was that Alauddin would free the Rana only if Padmini came to meet him. Padmini collected her wits and planned a Trojan horse ruse. She agreed to meet Allauddin, provided she was permitted to travel with her entourage of maids. As the train of decorated palanquins reached the Sultan's camp, there emerged, instead of royal maids, the fiercest of Rajput warriors. After a bloody battle, Rana Ratan Singh was freed. A cheated Alauddin renewed his siege and, in a final desperate stand, three thousand Rajput warriors died. When defeat seemed inevitable, Padmini and other women of the royal family committed *jauhar*. All Allauddin really won was a heap of ashes.

Yet, another legendary warrior of the house of Chittor was Rana Sangram

Singh. The hero of folklore, this battle-scarred fighter lost an eye and hand, but could still succeed in gathering Rajputs to fight Babur. Babur, who would ultimately lay the foundation of the Mughal Empire, won the battle by bringing to an end this last united stand of Hindu kings. As always, the Rajputs fought with courage, but they failed against Babur's superior strategy and earned his double-edged compliment, "The Rajputs know how to die in a battle but not how to win."

Mewar was the only Rajput kingdom never to bow to the Mughal might. Mewar fought again against Babur's grandson, Akbar, when Chittor fell to Mughal forces. Rana Pratap continued to defy the Mughals and when the two armies met again in the fields of Haldighati, Rana Pratap lost to the superior Mughal forces. He managed to escape into the Aravalli Hills, from where he continued to harass the Mughals. With the help of the Bhil tribes, he waged a successful guerilla war against Mughal domination till his death. Mewar's royal family gave to India its great spiritual poetess, the legendary Mira Bai, widow of Bhoj Raja and a passionate devotee of Lord Krishna. She moved out of the confines of the fort to wander through the land, composing and singing hymns in praise of Lord Krishna. Even today, her beautiful *bhajans* are sung by devotees.

No other Rajput kingdom offered such fierce resistance to the Mughals as Mewar. At a time, when numerous royal families of the country were striving to cultivate or enhance ties with the Mughals in Agra, Mewar was waging war against them. When other Rajput families offered their aunts, sisters, and daughters in marriage to the Mughal Emperor and his family, the people of Mewar refused to enter into an alliance with them, saying that these were families which had "diluted the Rajput seed" by marrying "foreign invaders". They preferred war to surrender, and hardship to dishonour. While the others bought peace and stability, Mewar suffered strife, hunger, and penury and persisted with its campaign against the Mughals. The purity of his descent and his strength of character had earned the head of the house of Mewar the title of *Hindua Suraj* or the Sun of the Hindus. He was accorded a high position of honour, and not just by the Hindus alone. Sir Alfred Lyall, a serving British officer, was at Bombay when the great Indian rulers came to welcome King Edward on his arrival in India. Talking to the famous minister of Hyderabad, Sir Alfred asked him of his keenness to meet the future king of England. Sir Salar Jung is said to have replied that there was one other person

The *katar*, a small but extremely useful weapon, is a part of a Rajput's armour, and is worn both at court and on the battlefield.

whom he longed to meet—the Maharana of Udaipur, who, for Indians, was the greatest of Indians.

The Rathors of Marwar, came from the ancient city of Kannauj. They trace their origins to the Sun and Lord Rama. After Jaichand lost his kingdom to Mohammed Ghori, the clan moved to the safety of the desert. Marwar's glory begins with Rao Jodha, who carved out an independent kingdom and founded its capital city of Jodhpur. The Rathors, ruled from the impregnable Mehrangarh Fort, which rises above the town atop a forbidding hill. Jodhpur's fortunes flourished, standing as it did astride the trade route connecting Asia to Europe. It became an important mercantile centre and, it is from here that the well-known trading community of Marwaris with their indomitable business acumen spread across India.

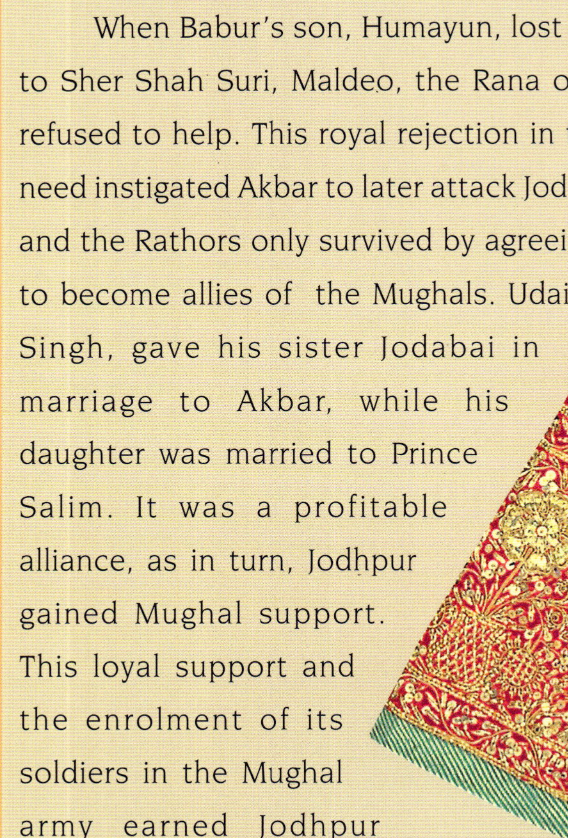

When Babur's son, Humayun, lost his kingdom to Sher Shah Suri, Maldeo, the Rana of Jodhpur refused to help. This royal rejection in time of need instigated Akbar to later attack Jodhpur and the Rathors only survived by agreeing to become allies of the Mughals. Udai Singh, gave his sister Jodabai in marriage to Akbar, while his daughter was married to Prince Salim. It was a profitable alliance, as in turn, Jodhpur gained Mughal support. This loyal support and the enrolment of its soldiers in the Mughal army earned Jodhpur rewards of both land and power. The most colourful among its kings, Jaswant Singh, changed sides many times during the battle of succession between the sons of Shah Jahan. Jaswant Singh's support for the different contenders among the four Mughal princes finally led to his defeat. His proud queen, incensed at his behaviour which she considered most dishonourable for a Rajput, is said to have slammed the gate of the fort in his face, refusing him entry. The relationship of the Mughals and the Rathors remained turbulent throughout the reign of Shah Jahan's son, Aurangzeb. After his death, the Rathors continued to play an active role in the court of the later Mughals. When the British arrived, Marwar signed a treaty with the East India Company and became one of the loyal princely states within the British Empire.

The Kachhwahas of Amber, trace their origins to Kush, the son of Lord Ram. They rose to great eminence through a fortuitous marriage alliance with Akbar. Raja Bhagwan Das gave his daughter in marriage to the Mughal emperor. She gave birth to Prince Salim, the heir-apparent, who later ascended the Mughal throne as Jahangir. These ties gave Amber a pre-eminent position among the Rajputs. The raja was rewarded with a command of 5000 horses and his successor, Man Singh, was not only one of Akbar's leading generals, but also a member of his close circle of confidants. Akbar trusted him so much that, during negotiations with Rana Pratap of Mewar, he sent Man Singh as his emissary. Rana Pratap refused to sit down to a meal with Man Singh and sent his son instead, showing his contempt for Amber's alliance with the Mughals. Both the Kachhwahas and the Mughals gained from the alliance as Akbar now had an dependable ally in this turbulent region. He also found safe passage to Ajmer to worship at the shrine of the Sufi saint Moinuddin Chishti. The Kachhwahas became fabulously rich through grants of land and acted as governors of Mughal provinces. And, as powerful generals, they led battalions in the Mughal army. Throughout the Mughal era they held positions of power and prestige, but paid for it with their independence, something which the house of Mewar never forgave them for. An illustrious Kachhwaha, was Sawai Jai Singh II who built the city of Jaipur. He moved his capital from the fortress of Amber to the plains below and built a brilliantly planned metropolis which became famous as the Pink City. He was also a keen astronomer

An exquisitely embroidered silk wedding skirt shows the rich taste and a great fondness for splendour.

and designed and constructed, huge astronomical observatories, "Jantar Mantar", at Jaipur, Delhi, and Varanasi.

The Rajputs are renowned for their sense of honour, pride, courage, and chivalry. However, history has shown that though they were great warriors they were incapable of forming a unified political force, even against invaders. Rajput clans stood aloof, failing to come to the aid of one another, even when their very survival was at stake. In spite of their martial talents, and their tradition of bravery, their power never extended beyond Rajasthan and they lost to a series of invaders. As a result, there were several famous and independent Rajput kingdoms, but never a Rajput "empire".

Under the influence of the Mughals, and then the British the Rajputs became increasingly partial to a grand lifestyle. They had a penchant for spending, and they ordered rather indiscriminately, objects d'art and furniture for their royal residences from Europe. The Maharaja of Jaipur favoured "Lalique crystal" dining and coffee tables. When Umaid Bhawan was being built in Jodhpur, the ship carrying the first consignment of furniture from England was bombed en route to India; a second order was placed, but the factory was burnt down so the Maharaja finally had the furniture copied by his own carpenters.

As forts became redundant, the Maharajas built themselves elaborate palaces as well as hunting lodges for *shikar*. A particularly good round of hunting with the Viceroy or other colonial administrators often gained them a number of concessions. The hunting lodges were equipped with all the trappings of a royal lifestyle — Rolls Royce cars were available, there was champagne at breakfast, and during *shikar*, a few cleverly placed marksmen behind the guests meant a particularly good haul which helped to enliven the atmosphere and keep the guests in a good mood. Alwar was known for its tiger hunts, Jodhpur for its pig-sticking, and Bikaner for its imperial sandgrouse shoots.

There was, a perpetual comparison of wealth versus the attributes of pride and honour, between the Rajput states. A poignant example of this was witnessed during the visit of Queen Elizabeth II to India during the early sixties. Culminating her state visit to India at Delhi, the Queen proceeded on a private visit to the states of Jaipur, Udaipur, and Banaras. During her visit to Jaipur, the Queen was accorded a tremendous reception befitting her status and her close family ties with Maharani Gayatri Devi and Maharaja Jai Singh of Jaipur. The hosts then presented the royal visitor an exquisite elephant carved out of a single emerald stone. Reports of these lavish festivities apparently put the Mewar court in a quandary. They could not match the wealth of their neighbours, yet they did not want to lose face. It was, then decided, to take recourse to the strictest tradition— the Queen was accorded a formal reception at the famous City Palace, where the Maharana and his Sardars, dressed in white, armed with swords and shields, and devoid of any traditional jewellery, greeted her. To match the emerald elephant, she was presented a reproduction in silver of the *Kirti Stambh*, the Tower of Victory, at Chittor. In more recent times, such rivalry can be witnessed at the polo grounds of Delhi and Jaipur.

This attitude, pleasantly attributed to a chip on the shoulder, is still prevalent in the present generation of the former ruling families. Arvind Singh, the Maharana, once recited a couplet in the local dialect. The verse, compared Amber Fort with Chittorgarh, explaining how the heart was filled with pride when one looked at Chittor, while on the other hand, one had to hang one's head in shame at the mere thought of Amber. This lampooned the policies of the State of Jaipur which had furthered its riches by alliances and marriages of convenience with the Mughals. Thus, the Fort of Amber had never been used for the purpose that it was built. On the other hand, The famous "Chitrakoot," as Chittorgarh is also known, symbolized the proud and chivalrous defiance of the Mewar populace. It was, as if, this comparison between the two neighbours would last another lifetime.

The British stealthily wove their way, into the internal affairs of the princely states. The Rajputs stayed loyal to them, and rejoiced when Queen Victoria was declared Empress of India and joined the Chamber of Princes. When India gained Independence in 1947, and then became a republic, the Rajput states were merged into the Indian Union and formed a part of the State of Rajasthan.

Gorgeous work of *darva* scanning and *Zari* embroidery add a touch of royal splendour to objects of utility and daily use.
Following page: The Rajput royalty, derived their love for fine dressing from the Mughal rulers. Their dresses in rich colours and elegant designs were embellished with embroidery.

Opposite page: Portrait of a young prince, wearing a gorgeous embroidered turban, ropes of pearls and *deaward,* silk dress — he has the making of a future ruler.

Top: The billiards room in the Lalgarh Palace, Bikaner is decorated with hunting trophies, tiger skins, stuffed heads of *barasinghas*, European *bric a brac*, and a colourful carpet. *Bottom:* The Lalgarh Palace, away from the confines of the Junagarh Fort palaces, is the modern residence of the Bikaner rulers, and was built by Maharaja Ganga Singh. It was designed by Sir Swinton Jacob in the early twentieth century. *Opposite page top:* Portraits of former rulers of Bikaner add a royal touch to the decor. *Opposite page bottom:* Throne room or Anup Mahal in the Junagarh Fort—the walls and ceiling are covered with elegant floral patterns and mirrors.

Exquisitely carved thrones were a matter of great pride for their owners, the maharajas.
Opposite page: Maharaja Bhawani Singh of Jaipur poses for a group photograph with other members of the royal family.
Preceding page: Princely beauties, part of the marriage entourage, take pleasure in watching the festivities.
Page 34-35: Royal marriages exude grandeur and ancient traditions, right from the wedding finery and jewellery, customs, processions to their royal magnificent palaces.

Dancing to their heart's delight, maidens of noble lineage participate in the royal pre- nuptial celebrations. *Opposite page top:* Handprints of the royal ladies who committed *sati,* or immolation by fire, as a tribute to the valour of their husbands who died on the battlefield. *Opposite page bottom:* Maharaja Bhawani Singh of Jaipur, celebrates the birthday of the princess, surrounded by royal ladies attired in traditional Rajasthani costumes and jewellery. *Following page:* A royal elephant that is used for grand processions and on ceremonial occasions — both social and religious. The ruler sat high in his seat from where he could be seen by the crowds. Within their private domestic circles the rulers performed religious *pujas* and ceremonies. The Maharaja of Jaipur performs a *puja* in the City Palace in Jaipur. *Page 44-45:* Occasions like Holi create scenes of sheer royal splendour. Huge crowds swarm the palace to pay respects to the royal family.

Forts and Palaces

One of the four doorways in the Pritam Chowk, City Palace, Jaipur, decorated with motifs depicting the four Indian seasons — here it is spring — flowers and flowers all the way. *Preceding page:* The Fort of Jaisalmer blessed by the hermit Eesul, was built by Jaisal of the Bhatti clan on Tricuta Hill in fulfilment of Lord Krishna's prophecy that a distant successor of his Lunar clan will establish his kingdom over the hill.

In Rajasthan, it is almost as if, every rocky outcrop gained its own fort and every lake a graceful palace. While the craggy, crenellated stone walls of the forts are a reminder of turbulent times, the graceful palace architecture recalls an era of luxurious ease. A Rajput saying defines a man as one who must, "in times of need wield a sword as well as at other times, write and design, with a pen and a brush." The Rajput warriors, lived up to this ideal. They created, a complete self-contained world within the protective walls of their hilltop citadels. Alongside the austere military quarters they built opulent palaces, temples, and pavilions decorated with delicate carvings and vivid frescoes.

Rajasthan was not always the "Place of Princes". The warring chiefs who raised these palaces and forts came to Marusthali—the Deathly Place — many centuries ago, riding at the head of wild marauding armies, that swept across the land, fragmenting it into innumerable fiefdoms. Given the violent chaos this resulted in, it wasn't long, before the first formidable fortifications with massive crenellated walls arose along hill tops, to define lines of defence. In some fortresses—such as Mehrangarh—parts of the walls, battlements, and embrasures were hewn directly from the rocky massif itself. In others, the very hills they crowned were burrowed into, creating dangerous maze-like warrens of tunnels, linked with one another to form escape routes to other fortresses and caches of plundered treasure.

As kingdoms expanded, and riches accumulated artisans were lured from far and near. Labour was locally stirred by feudal might and prisoners-of-war were put to work while fortunes were spent. Simple rock piles atop fortress hills began to be chiselled, dressed and fitted into mighty masonry walls and, as the raiders, inducted more horses into their evolving armies, stout gates were also put in. Ladders and battering-rams were created and, as the armies grew evermore inventive and powerful, the walls grew taller and the gates stronger. Bigger and better fortress walls were built around earlier walls and massive bastioned gateways were raised along pathways that twisted and turned to deny potential rammers a good run-up. Elephants coming around the bends, to bash in the gates with their foreheads, were dealt with, in turn, by cruel foot-long spikes driven directly into the doors. And, under siege, each seemingly impregnable gateway was to be held at all costs. Often, a total of seven gateways had to be crossed before the main fortress was reached.

In time, light catapults and then artillery came into the assault and answers in kind seemed logical from the forts. Alongside dozens of standard cannons, individual cannons were cast in gargantuan size. They were given fantastic titles and placed atop independent towers from which they could fling projectiles, weighing up to a full ton or more.

The tremendous thunderclap of these improbable war-pieces was, sometimes so great, that cannoneers were required to jump into surprisingly deep pits after lighting the wick, to save their own ear-drums. But still, with the arrival of such warfare there were mighty fortresses which fell to artillery barrages that sometimes went on for over thirty days.

Tragically, and yet also so heroically, it was routine amongst princes who found their fortresses on the verge of being taken by an enemy, to first consign all the women and children in the fort to flames. Then, the men all gathered together, and, charged-up with mind-numbing doses of opium, burst out of the gates to each take as many lives as they could in a last, madly suicidal, rush upon the enemy. Amongst members of the great princely dynasties, none was to ever remain alive to surrender, but their heirs were often smuggled out in such chaos.

Every fort in Rajasthan has been the scene of bloody battles, long sieges, intrigues, *jauhar* and surrender. Since the region was strategically placed near the border and through which important trade routes passed, it was attacked by almost every ruler who was ambitious to conquer North India. In Ranthambor Fort, a mass of crenellated walls and massive gateways, there is a tortuous, narrow path that leads up the hill to gigantic bastions, frowning ramparts, palaces, and temples. Among the most impressive buildings are a magnificent eighty-four-columned *chhatri*, an open columned pavilion, where King Hamir Deva held his royal audiences. The royal palace, with four underground storeys and the palaces of the royal seraglio as well as the two temples dedicated to Bhairon and Ganesh formed part of the complex. Impregnable, the fort was never taken in straight battle. It only fell to treason and intrigue. The indelible marks of cannon balls and the songs sung by bards recall, in a verbal imagery the suicidal courage displayed by kings and soldiers.

Chittorgarh has mammoth ramparts with imposing battlements, raised as if to challenge the might of other kings. It was attacked in vengeful fury by Alauddin Khalji when, his ruses failed to subdue Queen Padmini. It was conquered by the Sultan of Gujarat after a desperate resistance from the Rajputs led by Queen Karnavati. It was subsequently wrested from Gujarat and returned to the Guhilot rulers by Humayun, then attacked again by Akbar, furious at Chittor's failure to offer sanctuary to his father when he was in trouble. Akbar's successor, Jahangir returned Chittorgarh to Mewar's rulers on condition that the broken walls must not be repaired.

Every building, within the fort has its own history. The *chhatri* is a memorial to the brave warriors, Jaimal and Phatta, who died fighting. The *Vijay Sthambha*, the victory tower, a renowned symbol of Chittor stands tall for all to admire. In the vaults, Queen Padmini and her royal ladies walked stoically into the flames, preferring this act of *jauhar*, to captivity. The walls are still charred black with the smoke resulting from this tragic episode, but the palace

Patwon-ki-Haveli is one of the finest examples of the most exquisite craftsmanship on stone — a jeweller's art has been practised on the carving. *Following page:* A window covered with a glass mosaic, depicting gorgeous peacocks and flowers—the light filtering through the panel creates fascinating patterns.

of Padmini, still stands beside a beautiful pool.

However, within the secure defensive walls of the forts, luxuries, pomp, and ostentation also found a place. Fortresses were divided into service areas, pleasure areas, court areas, and family areas. Fabulous palaces were built for favoured queens, princes, and princesses. Some were raised high to just enjoy the desert air and take in the fabulous view, others, were created on pure whim. Airy halls were named for Victory, the Wind, and the Clouds and they were sculpted into architectural effulgence of towers, canopies, kiosks, windows and battlements. Gardens were laid out, with fountains of fragrant waters and bedrooms were plastered with fragments of mirrors set into a mortar of crushed mother-of-pearl. The rooftop "Wind Palaces", were rigged up to simulate rain, even in the fiercest heat of summer. Meanwhile, for the conduct of more mundane affairs, grand halls were erected to serve as public or private audience halls, allowing accessible and yet appropriately regal stances to be held before subjects, the nobility, envoys, and other princes.

Junagarh Fort, Bikaner's main citadel, encompasses a world of sheer splendour. It has opulently decorated palaces and landscaped gardens as well as pavilions. The small, Badal Mahal, has blue rain clouds pierced with streaks of lightning painted on the walls and ceiling. The gorgeous Anup Mahal or the Diwan-i-Khas has gold and scarlet floral motifs covering every inch of the surface with the royal throne placed majestically, in the centre. Floral motifs, images of deities and stained glass decorations create an aura of luxury in the Phool Mahal and Chandra Mahal, both, palaces for the women. Here can be seen Rao Bika's bed, low enough, to prevent any assassin from hiding beneath. A terrace pavilion, decorated with lavish ornamentation, with murals depicting Krishna's dalliance with milkmaids and a million flowers blooming create a beautiful, natural fantasy. A huge, brocade hand-drawn fan, is woven with peacock motifs, and hangs from the ceiling over the small bed. The showpiece of Junagarh is a sandalwood throne, believed to be the oldest piece of furniture in India, dating back to the fifth century CE. Some distance from Junagarh Fort stands, the red sandstone Lalgarh Palace with its finely-carved stone screens. It was built by Maharaja Ganga Singh in the twentieth century and was designed by the British architect, Swinton Jacob.

Within the impregnable Meherangarh Fort at Jodhpur, is the jewel-like Phool Mahal palace, embellished with frescoed ceilings, richly painted with brilliant colours and highlighted in gold. Such an ambience of luxury, is further enhanced by the rare, stained-glass windows and mirrors. A museum, housing a unique collection of artefacts has, on display, the only surviving "original" Mughal tent. Made of red silk and velvet and embroidered with gold *zari* work, it was the treasured possession of the "Grand Mogul", Emperor Shah Jahan. Raja Jaswant Singh of Jodhpur plundered it from Aurangzeb's camp. An outstanding collection, musical instruments, palanquins, elephant howdahs, royal costumes and furniture are well-preserved. Old cannons in a daunting array, stand guard over the city. They are mounted on the ramparts, looking down on Jodhpur, beyond which stretch endless vistas of the desert.

The Udaipur City Palace is, a royal residence which has been expanded, over the centuries. The original core is around the courtyard or Raj Angan. Successive rulers, each added a wing. Yet, these extensions to the palace, built in different styles of architecture and ornamentation, blend with a surprising harmony and elegance. The coronations of the Guhilot rulers were always held in the Chandra Mahal. In the Dilkusha Mahal, a suite of four seventeenth century rooms is enchantingly decorated with both glass tiles and murals. Bari Mahal, built around a courtyard atop a twenty-seven-metre high hill has been the stage for all the festive celebrations of the royal household. A flight of steep, narrow stairs, go down and up again to bring you to the Krishna Vilas a small apartment decorated with exquisite miniature paintings in the authentic Mewar style. The splendid "Peacock Courtyard" is where *durbars* were held. It has a gorgeous glass mosaic in stucco, depicting the dazzling plumage of the peacock. Among other palaces the most picturesque are Jag Mandir and Jag Niwas, built on islands in the Pichola Lake. These palaces can be seen from every window of the City Palace, framed like images of a royal fantasy.

The later palaces, at Amber Fort, were built in an extravagant style, to rival Mughal grandeur and opulence. As a matter of fact, when Jahangir came to visit Amber, the double row of elephant-headed brackets at the Diwan-i-Am had to be covered in stucco to avoid displeasing the emperor. Entry to the royal residential area is through the magnificent Ganesh Pol, which is lavishly covered with elegant frescoes and crowned with pavilions and delicate screens. The rooftop pavilion or Diwan-i-Khas, is decorated with hundreds of prismatic mirrors and is a showpiece in itself. Raja Man Singh's palaces for the women of his court are the oldest buildings in the fort. A *baradari*, an open garden pavilion, stands in a central courtyard surrounded by private apartments with frescoes depicting scenes from the Krishna Leela.

In Jaipur, the new capital of the Kachhwahas was one

of the first planned cities of India. The City Palace, stands at the centre of the metropolis. The entrance to the original residence of Sawai Jai Singh, Chandra Mahal, is through a magnificent gateway with splendid brass studded doors which are guarded by a pair of elephants carved in white marble. On display in the Diwan-i-Khas, are two gigantic silver urns used by Madho Singh II to carry Ganga Jal, holy water from the Ganga, on board the ocean liner when he travelled to London. These urns, are the largest silver vessels in the world, weighing 242 kilos, and holding 8182 gallons of water. The Palace Museum has an excellent collection of miniature paintings as well as palanquins, manuscripts, textiles, costumes and Persian carpets. The four small doors in the stately courtyard are painted with motifs that depict the four seasons. Chandra Mahal is seven-storeyed, and topped by the Mukut Mandir, an elegant pavilion with a curvilinear "Bengal" roof. Each floor has been decorated, in different styles, to suit individual tastes. For example, the Chini Niwas has been painted in "Wedgewood" blue with white patterns.

The Hawa Mahal or the Palace of Winds is a prominent landmark of the city of Jaipur. A five-storeyed facade, with 953 niches and trellised screens has been built at one end of the women's palace. This intriguing structure, has the depth of a single room. The royal ladies could sit, here in seclusion, and watch the city, at the same time enjoy the cool breeze. Hence the name, "Palace of Winds." A winding ramp takes you to the top for a bird's eye view of the city and Nahargarh Fort. The Hawa Mahal is sheer architectural fantasy, "Alladin's magician could have been called into existence no more marvellous abode", wrote Sir Edwin Arnold.

When the mighty Mughals and the British arrived, the princes of Rajasthan gradually succumbed to the domination of the empires. As wars became less frequent, a new sense of "luxurious" security spread through the old Deathly region. The princes of Rajasthan were, at last lured, out of their high hill-fortresses, onto the hitherto forbidden plains. The princes and their families had accumulated wealth and, they were assured of great incomes. They enjoyed the power to indulge their every whim, and had armies of rich and powerful subjects and servitors at their feet. There were rambunctious festivals and religious occasions, massive hunts involving entire armies, regal celebrations, processions, competitions, and games. In addition, there were ostentatious state visits and marriages—ranging from the wildly romantic to the coldly diplomatic—between great dynasties.

Longer spells of peace and an ensured prosperity, lured the princes towards self-indulgence. Settled into their luxurious palaces and surrounded by servitors, they wrote poetry, quaffed opium, smoked narcotic herbs or drank "potent" and supposedly "aphrodisiac" liquors made from precious metals and the mashed brains of animals, between visits into the parallel universe of the harems comprising their many queens,

Still surviving is the frescoed splendour of the Rang Mahal in the Samode Palace near Jaipur. The paintings depict religious themes as well as royal portraits and vie with the best known examples of painting.

princesses and of course, concubines. For deep in the palaces were these ladies, each often heir to a delicate female lineage of beauty, nubility, intelligence and grace. A lineage as noble, heroic and bold as that of their princely brothers and fathers, and the husbands they were each expected to eventually die for. They bore and brought up their progeny, the princes of the future. Like luxuriously indulged queen-bees, in the centre of their respective colossal hives. Hidden throughout their lives far from the view of strangers and men other than their own, they surveyed all the goings-on of the palaces from behind peepholes, stone trellises, curtains, and secret corridors. Favoured by the king, who listened to them, it was often one of these princesses, who, in actuality, held the true reins of power in the kingdom.

In what seemed like a single, convulsive act of glory, in their histories of greatness — the princes of Rajasthan went on an exuberant building-spree, erecting new palaces in new locations, each more fabulous than the next. Flamboyant, Indo Saracenic fusions, with art-deco embellishments. The design of the structures ranged from 'Raj' fantasies to heavy, straightforward British Civic. They sprung up as though they were great dynasties, that were to rise to even greater glory. No expense or effort was spared: massive rooms and corridors were constructed to house the most expensive indulgences in the world. Considerations for security were boiled down to formal guards at formal gates. The armies were lent out in the service of the overlords, the British, or maintained just for show, and for the hunt.

The Umaid Bhawan Palace was built as a "famine relief project" giving employment to the needy. Umaid Singh commissioned British architect and designer H.V. Lancaster to effect the programme. The huge central dome of Umaid Bhawan is 59.4 metres high. The central marble hall, has ornate balconies and sweeping staircases as well as ceilings with sold inlay and parquet floors. Unique, the palace is a blend of traditional Indian architecture and luxurious European interiors. This gives it its own distinctive character. While the red sandstone domes and arches are Indian in style, the rooms and swimming pool are decorated in the Beaux Art and Art Deco style of early twentieth-century Europe.

Some of the palatial residences of the maharajas have, today, been converted into exotic-luxury hotels. These have captured the imagination of the visitors who get a first-hand feel of royal living. The outstanding ones are the Lake Palace in Udaipur, Rambagh Palace in Jaipur and Umaid Bhawan in Jodhpur. They are rated amongst the best hotels in the world. A multitude of ancestral homes, have been restored and converted into heritage hotels. Deep in the desert, with stony hills as the backdrop, the Samode Palace dazzles the eye. It was here, that the entire epic, *The Far Pavilions*,

The Jaivan Cannon in the Jaigarh fort overlooking the Amber Palace was made by the cannon foundry within the fort itself. This mammoth cannon with a twenty-feet long barrel is the largest wheeled cannon in the world.
Following page: Magnificent view of Jodhpur city lying under the ramparts of the fort. The city is pierced by a gigantic spur of mighty rock on which is built the Mehrangarh fort.

was shot. Samode's 400-year-old palace has, perhaps, the most extravagant murals and mirror-work ornamentation in Rajasthan. The builders covered every available surface with gold leaf and paint to create an ambience of unparalleled opulence. Sultan Mahal, Darbar Hall, and Sheesh Mahal are covered with lavish mirror-work decorations on stucco and portraits of deities, damsels, and dancers of charm and beauty.

Far out in the desert, slumbering Jaisalmer, is a town straight out of the pages of history. Few know that Satyajit Ray, the Oscar-winning film-maker, used Jaisalmer Fort as the backdrop for one of his films. The citadel has been rechristened, *Sonar Qila* or Golden Fort after the golden-hued sandstone used in its structure. Within its walls are charming palaces and *havelis*, the mansions of the wealthy. The ornate Patwon-ki-Haveli and Nathmal-ki-Haveli have outer walls covered with intricately carved lattice screens glowing a delicate golden pink when caught in the afternoon sunshine. The uppermost pavilions are embellished with exquisite murals, depicting nautch girls, hunting scenes, and landscapes. From these small apartments is visible, a stunning view of Jaisalmer city, surrounded by a "sea" of sand. Unlike most forts of the region, Jaisalmer is still inhabited, almost a quarter of the town's population live within its walls.

The Rajputs excelled in stone carving and created fascinating facades of unparalleled artistry. Seen here are panels of filigreed screens that form the upper portion of a *zenana* quarters in the Lalgarh Palace, Bikaner.
Opposite page: Hawa Mahal in Jaipur, the most exquisitely designed palace of winds, was built for the royal women — it allowed them to watch processions on the road protected from the gaze of the common man. *Preceding page:* The Mehrangarh Fort, standing proudly atop the 125 metre high hill, commands the most spectacular view for miles around it.

The *havelis* of Shekhawati contain some of the most spectacular painted facades and interiors, depicting horses and elephants and many other contemporary scenes from day-to-day life. *Opposite page:* This doorway in the Pritam Chowk, City Palace, Jaipur celebrates the rainy season and depicts the peacock in its gorgeous plumage. This door leads to the Diwan-i-am or public audience courtyard of the palace. *Page 70-71:* Umaid Bhawan, the largest private residence in the world, was built as a famine relief project by Maharaja Umaid Singh. Royal vintage cars, a symbol of modernity, stand parked in front of the magnificent palace in Jodhpur.

The walls, windows, and ceiling of the Anoop Mahal in the Junagarh Fort, Bikaner create a world of extraordinary charm and splendour. *Opposite page:* An exquisite example of inlay craft for which the Rajasthani craftsmen have achieved world wide reputation. The door, the pillars and the floor are extremely charming specimens of local art and craft. *Following page:* The royal seat in red velvet, and the umbrella were gifted to the Jodhpur rulers by Shahjahan. Darbar Takhat, where this seat is placed, is the Diwan-i-Aam, or the hall of public audience in the Mehrangarh Fort, Jodhpur.

U.S.7852 ★
16

17

A Desert Land and its People

A gigantic multi-layered turban adorns the head of a Rajasthani man, who is very proud of his headgear, a symbol of his status in his village and place in society. *Preceding page:* According to a custom, the womenfolk eat in complete privacy, covered by a colourful *odhni,* cotton shawl, away from the eyes of the menfolk. Rajasthani village folk still practise traditional customs.

In Rajasthan, itinerant bards raise their voices, singing in fulsome praise: *Marudhar maharo desh mhane bhalo lage ji*, the desert, my country, I love you.

In this land of kings, myths and legends, are inextricably woven into the everyday life of the people. Bards, even today, sing of the exploits of the valiant, death-defying Rajputs and their proud, determined women. Every square centimetre of this sun-kissed, battle-scarred land lies steeped in romance and chivalry, history and legend. The people's love of vibrant colours reflects their irrepressible zest for living. The monochromatic hues of the desert are relieved by splashes of dazzling colours—the blue and magenta of a woman's veil and swaying skirt, or the orange and red of the man's turban setting the sand dunes ablaze. With dignity and pride, the people of the harsh desert defy every hardship—living in tiny hamlets, surrounded by an endless sea of shifting sand. They are extraordinarily talented craftsmen, with an innate sense of design, evident in the simplest objects of daily use. They also create a rich variety of textiles and ornate leatherware. The building of forts and palaces and the continual demands of a royal lifestyle also gave rise to highly skilled artisans who worked with finesse.

A beaten path meanders it's way to the palace that adorns the crest of the hill. Familiar scents and sounds rise from the village that lies sprawled below — the smell of camels and woodsmoke, of water on parched ground and spiced food cooking on charcoal fires—the chatter and laughter of children at play, and the lilting folk songs are a background to the beehive hum of everyday living.

In the arid landscape, in its dusty and yet profusely colourful, alive and serpentine bylanes, Rajasthan unfolds its fourth dimension. It is a mood and rhythm so overpowering, that even the most seasoned traveller is caught unawares. Rajasthan haunts like a dream, it is a land that continues to breathe, the fire of the pomp and pageantry of yesteryears. A land of bloody battles and forbidden passions.

The state is truncated by the jagged Aravalli range one of the oldest mountain ranges in the world. The hues of the mountains are inspiring, gleaming flame in the dawn light and a blaze of silver at midday, it dons a cloak of gold and rose at sunset which deepens to lilac and lavender at dusk.

The last scattered ridges of the Aravallis are found in Delhi. The Delhi-Jaipur highway has an excellent view of the approach to the Aravallis. Elsewhere, its hilltops in Chittorgarh, Kotah, Bundi, Amer, and Kumbhalgarh are fortified with magnificent citadels, the stones mutely testifying to tales of intrigue and battles lost and won.

The Aravallis divide this land of the Rajputs into two distinct regions: one, dominated by scrub and thorn, a restless scape of shifting sands, the forbidding

Following page: A Rajasthani woman goes to work, carrying tools of her profession on her head and works hard for her living. Ivory or plastic bangles cover a large part of her arm and protect her skin from the harsh sun.
Page 78-79: Traditional Rajasthani men wear dazzling - white *dhotis*, jackets and *mojris*, leather sandals. The turban, worn on their head is a showpiece. It is always in gorgeous rainbow colours—red, pink, bright yellow, blue or green.
Page 80-81: Women drying their colourful clothes after a bath in the holy Pushkar during the Kartik poornima festival.

Thar Desert; the other verdant, fertile, and rich in mineral deposits. Every hill and stream carries its own ancient tale. Even the Thar Desert, with its endless stretches of sand, that occupy most of western Rajasthan, has inspired the people to weave their own myths around it. Legend says Lord Rama, hero of the epic *Ramayana* enroute to rescue Sita, kidnapped and held captive by the ten-headed wicked Ravana, was barred safe passage over the ocean dividing Bharat or India from Lanka. Rama, with his divine powers, energised an arrow endowing it with the power to dry up the ocean. The threat of this divine weapon quelled all resistance. Rama could then cross safely. But the arrow powered by an irrevocable *mantra* had to find a target. Destiny ordained the Saraswati River as Rama's target. The river dried up, the verdure disappeared, and golden sand swept over vast reaches. For the more prosaic, scientific mind, the legendary Saraswati was, in fact, vanquished by earthquakes, diverting its course inevitably, leaving a dry and barren region. Today only a few stray streams survive in the Thar. They are seasonal streams which swell during the rains and dry into deep river beds in the summer. The mighty Saraswati is, but a memory. Archaeological finds indicate this was once a green and fertile land.

Rajasthan covers an area of 342,274 square kilometres, divided by the low rolling hills of the Aravalli Range. North and west, around Bikaner, Jaisalmer, and Jodhpur, arid plains begin and then the desert appears. The Aravalli Hills protect the rest of the state from the relentless advance of sand. Making up for the loss of the Saraswati are the living rivers. The Luni runs its course from Ajmer to the Rann of Kutch. The Banas and the Chappan flow eastwards from their stream-fed source in the Aravallis. The Chambal is the only perennial river in all of Rajasthan. However, there are, large magnificent lakes, many of them man made, which keep the land fertile.

Moving westwards from the Gangetic plain, the region around Jaipur is verdant, as it falls in the path of the monsoons. Here, farmlands are interspersed by forests of mesquite and *dhak* trees. But as you cross the low hills of the Aravallis, the landscape begins to change. Few touches of green on the rocky hills of granite and sandstone come from low spreading *amla* and *kejri* trees, the fertile farmlands give way to smaller arid patches. Going even further westwards beyond Jodhpur and then to Jaisalmer, sand dunes appear on the horizon. This is *marusthali*, the land of death, the great golden Thar. Home only to the thorny *babul*, growing from the stony ground, the most precious commodity being clear, sweet water. Across the Thar, slow-moving camel packs imprint their tracks across shifting sands and huge balls of dried grass are blown by strong dust-laden winds. This region is very ancient and a great civilization once existed here even as early as five thousand years ago, before the Aryans arrived in the Indian subcontinent. Excavations near the banks of the River Banas and its tributaries reveal traces of human habitation as old as the palaeolithic period. The best preserved archaeological site in Rajasthan is the pre-Harappan city of Kalibangan, near Bikaner. In the hierarchy of well-known sites it follows Mohenjodaro and Harappa as the third largest city of (Cerca 3000 BCE) the Indus Valley Civilization, thriving in the region. At Kalibangan, excavations reveal plain and painted pottery, copper implements, terracotta figurines, and seals bearing the legendary Harappan pictograms.

The Aryans arrived on horseback and in armoured chariots, flaunting their awesome power and changing the course of history. Exhibiting traces of their supposed East European origins, they were blue-eyed, fair-haired and fair-skinned; they drank heavily and worshipped with hymns and sacrifice the sun, the wind, water, and fire. Cattle breeding was their main occupation, which gradually turned to farming. A pastoral people, nomadic by a need, to search for fertile pastures. They used force, to gain cattle grazing territory. They are believed to have originated, from Central Asia and moved to Persia and regions around the Caspian Sea. They swept in hordes through the mountain passes of the Hindu Kush raising havoc. Peaceful Harappan settlements, unable to face this onslaught were vanquished. The people sought safety, by moving southwards, beyond the hills, abandoning their land to the more martial Aryans.

Historically, the martial tradition is the foremost feature of this region. Having descended from the Aryan warrior-tribes of Central Asia, the people of Rajasthan echo the characteristics of their origins. Arthur Basham, the widely-read historian, observed that "the invaders were from mixed tribes, and descended in numerous waves over many centuries, speaking various Indo-European languages." The settlements grew, the very presence of such varied races brought about the creation of a more structured social system. Gradually, society became divided into groups according to occupation, based on the four *varnas* or castes namely *brahmin*, *kshatriya*, *vaisya*, and *sudra*.

The Minas, a legendary tribe, exemplify the image of fierce warriors and loyal soldiers. Traditionally, they are retainers of the Rajput royal houses and are believed to be descendants of the original Harappan people. The Susawat Minas who ruled the Dhundhar Valley were defeated by the Kachhwahas in the early tenth century and became retainers of the royal family of Amber. Bound, by an iron code of loyalty, and an ability to keep secrets, they were deservedly appointed custodians of Amber's vast treasures kept hidden at Jaigarh Fort. Legend has it, only the Mina guardians know exactly where these fabulous treasures are hidden. Not even members of the royal family are aware of the location. Even today, a Mina chief is ceremonially accorded a place of honour at the coronation of a Kachhwaha ruler. The Bhils, another prominent tribe, nomadic and great fighters, remain feared for their mastery over the bow and arrow and ability to fight in the hills. Aryan invaders overcame them and they retreated, settling in remote areas. Bhil characters appear in the *Ramayana* where Shabri, a poor Bhil woman, offers berries to Rama. In the *Mahabharata*, Eklavya, a Bhil boy, was refused archery lessons by Dronacharya and later Krishna was killed at Dwarka by the arrow of a Bhil hunter.

The Gadia Lohars, as their name proclaims, are nomadic ironsmiths. These turbaned men and, women in flaring skirts, are a familiar sight in numerous towns in northern India. They travel in their ornate iron carts, camping on the outskirts of a village or town where fires are lit to make iron implements for farmers and carpenters. Legend has it, when Chittor was lost by the Mewar king Rana Pratap to Akbar, they vowed never to return till the Guhilots ruled again. As it so happened the Guhilots chose to build a new capital at Udaipur and did not return to Chittor. Firm in their resolve, the Gadias have pursued the role of wandering nomads. In recent times, they have refused all offers of land. The late Prime Minister,

Jawaharlal Nehru, attempted to resettle them, but to no avail. The Banjaras, another colourful nomadic tribe, trace their lineage to the Yadav clan of Lord Krishna. Historically, they trade in salt and helped Alexander the Macedonian cart off his booty from India. The Mughals used them as camp followers to cart luggage and as pathfinders when they headed southwards across Rajasthan. The Bishnois, a justly renowned ethnic group, living between Jodhpur and Bikaner, maintain a unique tradition as passionate conservationists. They regard the deer as sacred and their efforts for the preservation of trees has won them worldwide attention. Bishnois have sacrificed lives to protect their beloved trees and animals. Today, a Bishnoi settlement is a green, fertile oasis in the sands of the Thar, surrounded by forests inhabited by deer and peacocks.

Amongst the most popular ways of exploring the wonders of Rajasthan, for an experience yet unparalleled, is the splendid luxury train, The Palace on Wheels. Having qualified among the "Ten Best Train Journeys" of the world. For, not only does it offer a holiday tour, tailor-made for a romantic escapade, it brings alive the romance of Rajasthan and gives travellers an opportunity to feel like royalty—for a week.

It is easy to sink into the opulence of the Palace on Wheels, to the rhythm of the gently rocking train that takes one through a mesmerising 'sight-see by day and travel by night' guided tour. The party begins with passengers checking in at Delhi Cantonment's railway station, from where the train commences its circuitous route with guests receiving fragrant garlands and a shower of petals from beaming attendants. Over the next seven nights and eight days, pit-stops are made at Chittorgarh, Udaipur, Jaisalmer, Jodhpur, Bharatpur and Bikaner before returning to Delhi.

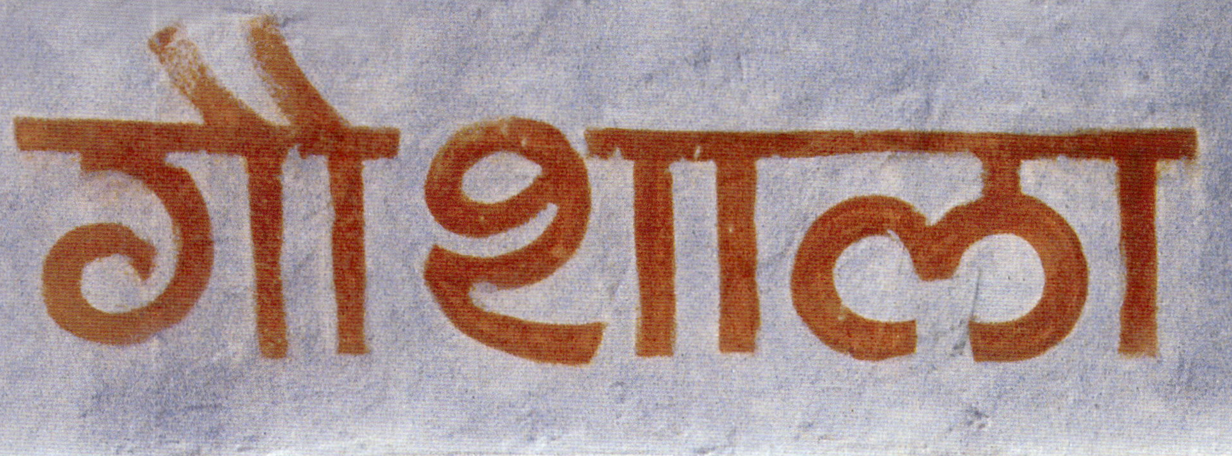
गौशाला

A woman steps out of her door to welcome a guest. The jewellery, bangles, necklaces and a silver ornamental ball on the forehead create a picture of tasteful elegance. *Opposite page:* The doors of the simple, unpretentious dwellings are ornamented with floral motifs. Leaves are painted in green to symbolize the richness of their hearts and profundity of nature which is wanting in the desert. *Preceding page:* Rajasthan is a land of spectacular colour. The colours of the village women's attire are extremely vibrant and symbolize the strength of their character and vividly contrast with the monochromatic dullness of the desert.

Menfolk are no less keen to demand attention for their impeccable dressing. White dhotis, shirts, jackets and of course the magnificent turbans in traditional Rajasthani *bandhni,* tie and dye. *Opposite page:* "Of old unhappy far off things and battles long ago" — the musician couple on the steps of the Patwon ki haveli in Jaisalmer, play on the double-stringed *ravanhatta.* They sing ballads, celebrating the heroism of legendary warriors and the eternal love of Dhola and Maruni.

The huge moustaches and the splendid ear ornaments set this Rajasthani villager apart in a crowd of men. His ferocity stems from hardships but his heart is of pure gold. *Opposite page:* The woman is undisturbed by the camera. She knows she is beautiful, her jewellery is eye - catching and her dress is gorgeous — she is a picture of unaffected beauty. *Following page:* The camel is the most prized possession of a villager in Rajasthan. In fact, the camel is the only means of transport across the desert areas of western Rajasthan.

"Do take our photographs"— these youngmen seem to ask, and why not—the splendid arrogance of their turbaned heads is so distinctive and charming. They are relaxed and spontaneous all the way. *Opposite page:* A Rajasthani woman is noted for her love of finery, clothes, and jewellery. Unmindful of the curious onlookers, she flaunts her silver anklets.

Women in their finery await the arrival of the groom, as they look curiously from the balcony over a courtyard decorated with festoon.
Opposite page: A Rajasthani man is quite a "peacock" in his dressing. The turban tying is not a simple art and only the most adept fingers can accomplish the perfection of form.
Following page: The shepherds raise their cattle in the quite and peace of their village environment—far from the maddening crowd.
Page 98-99: Dancing is a way of life in the desert. Women dressed in red odhnis collectively join together in the folk dance, while a group of spectators looks on.
Page *100-101:* The camel, justly called the ship of the desert, is the only means of transport to the interiors of the land that is covered with dunes and thorny bushes.

Fairs and Festivals

The Pushkar fair is the place where people from villages make their annual purchases ranging from women's cosmetics to trinkets for decorating their most precious possession— their camels.
Preceding page: Pushkar, the cattle and camel fair in Rajasthan is the largest of its kind. It draws thousands of village folk and people from neighbouring states. This two-day fair, over the sacred lake, is an unforgettable experience.

As women dance to the intricate drum beats, their voluminous, gathered skirts, swirl out like the blossoming petals of a flower. Then, men with fierce moustaches and kohl-lined eyes, brandish swords and sticks, as they dance to martial rhythms. For the villagers of Rajasthan, life can be very hard, as they battle the relentlessness of the desert. Festivals are a reprieve, a time to abandon themselves to dancing the *ghoomar* and the *teratali*, sing folk songs, and visit the bright stalls selling everything from trinkets and ribbons, to cooking pots and leatherware.

The fairs of Rajasthan are a combination of religious rituals, commerce, and fun. Most fairs are centred around a temple festival and provide an opportunity for traders to sell their wares to visitors. Dancers and musicians, puppeteers and minstrels along with other entertainers frequent the fairs. The fairs commence, with prayers at the temple, a dip in a sacred water body, followed by a burst of happy festivity—new clothes, meeting people, and feasting. Colourful stalls spring up, like magic among the sand dunes. Fluttering with veils and ribbons, and bright with jewellery. Everything is sold here from textiles and bangles to furniture and folk paintings. These fairs, often camel and cattle fairs, offer a good selection of local handicrafts. One corner dazzles with bright neon lights where the circus, Ferris wheel, and magic shows take place and at another, food stalls entice the visitor, with the heady aroma of food.

The cattle fair at Pushkar, held in November, is Rajasthan's most popular fair. Pushkar is separated in the city of Ajmer by the Nag Pahar Hill and its Brahma Temple. The temple, is one of the holiest pilgrimages, for the Hindus. Pushkar has three lakes, Jyeshtha, Madhya, and Kanishtha Pushkar and a dip in the Jyeshtha Lake assures a place in heaven—no further penance, or austerities are required to attain divine bliss. Later, in order to restrict the overflowing number of entrants to heaven it was ordained that a dip in the lake must be taken during the five days before Kartik P*urnima*, the full moon in November. The Jyeshtha Pushkar lake has fifty-two bathing *ghats* built by the royal families of Rajasthan and one built by Queen Mary of England. Behind the stone steps of the *ghats* rise, brilliantly white-washed temples and rest houses for the pilgrims. The Brahma Temple is the focal point and is built above a stately flight of steps. The fair is held for five days, when the place is inundated by pilgrims. It is the largest cattle fair in the world and there is feverish bargaining over the price of camels and horses. Village folk camp out in the sand dunes in elaborately decorated carts with their camels proudly looking over the colourful multitudes. Acres of sand dunes are dotted with the bivouacs of camel herders and cowherds, their livestock scattered everywhere. Quaint circuses raise their big-tops alongside raucously clattering joy-rides driven by devilish machines chugging out clouds

The Gangaur festival in Rajasthan celebrates the union of Shiva and Parvati and invokes divine blessings for marital bliss. Images of the Lord and his consort, are taken out in a procession along the main roads of Jaipur — women dressed in bridal costumes and elaborate jewellery turn out to seek blessings in ever-swelling numbers.

of black smoke. The streets are cordoned to serve as bazaars where stalls seemingly tumble over each other in a chaotic bonhomie. They peddle everything, from a poor Indian farmer's most basic needs to the most extravagant 'kitsch'. In keeping with the times, peanut fields and gooseberry orchards are let out to serve as acres of tented mini-cities for the most privileged—but none find space in Pushkar's famous rose farms.

With rows of trucks standing by, buyers of livestock strut about the sands in immaculately white traditional dress, always distinct from the inescapably dusty looks of those that have trudged across miles of desert to sell the camels, bulls, and cows. Young horse-breeders wax moustaches into fierce black scimitars across their cheeks and charge around, all over the place, showing off their stock. Village children tag onto tourists, show them around and brush-up on their English, French, or Italian. Meanwhile, weary westerners are taken around in camel-carts, bristling with cameras and water-bottles—burnt red as tomatoes by the blazing sun—while others, adjust to the ambience and delightedly wander about for hours on foot. Many camel races and other competitions are held, and folk dancers as well as musicians perform alongside magicians and acrobats. In the evening, the mood shifts to the devotional. The lakes lie under a thick fog, as groups of pilgrims sing devotional *bhajans* and float earthen lamps in the still, dark-waters. From the temple, the blowing of conch shells and the ringing of bells float down along with incense that perfumes the air. For the believer, Brahma is present at Pushkar to listen to the prayers.

The *dargah* or shrine of the Sufi saint Khwaja Muinuddin Chishti at Ajmer is where the largest *Urs* celebration takes place. It attracts pilgrims from all across the Islamic world. An *Urs* commemorates the death of a Sufi saint. There are no religious distinctions made at the shrine adding to its immense popularity with Hindus. Sheikh Muinuddin was a direct descendant of Prophet Mohammed. He was a disciple of the Sufi saint, Khwaja Usman Haruni and he acquired, great spiritual knowledge. The Chauhan rulers of Ajmer welcomed him and he founded the Chishtia order in India. After his death, the *dargah* became the spiritual centre of the Sufis. Akbar was a regular visitor to the *dargah* as were many other emperors and kings. Lying below the Taragarh Fort hill, the simple brick structure of the original tomb has received various additions over centuries. Akbar built a red sandstone mosque, while, the gold pinnacles above the dome, were added by the Nawab of Rampur. The gateway, known as the Buland Darwaza, was built by a Sultan of Mandu and Emperor Jahangir is said to have added gold railings, which are now replaced by silver ones. Shahjahan built a marble mosque while, his daughter, the Mughal princess Jahanara, added the courtyard called Begami Dalan. The *mehfilkhana*, was a gift of the Nizam of Hyderabad. The immense cauldrons where food is cooked for devotees were originally jointly gifted by Akbar and Jahangir.

During the Urs the *dargah* complex is transformed into a mammoth fair. All the lanes leading to it throng with crowds that surge towards the inner sacred precincts. Small kiosks sell *henna*, perfume, kohl, silver and gold thread or *zari* and trinkets. Eating houses serve delectable *kababs* and *biryani*. The air is laden with the heady fragrance of incense, perfume and tons of rose petals. And, there are echoes of the chanting of verses from the *Quran*. Countless shops mushroom around the *dargah* selling the richly embroidered *chadars*, sheets that are offered at the *mazhaar*, the grave of the saint. The *khadims*, at the *dargah*, are the service men, who wander about guiding pilgrims. Sometimes one sees dancing dervishes in their billowing garments and bead necklaces holding peacock feathers and swirling to the beat of the drums. The Sajjada-nashin, the head of the *dargah*, sits in the Begami Dalan on the *gaddi*, the seat of the *khwaja* or saint, blessing and guiding the stream of pilgrims. The *mehfilkhana* resounds with the devotional songs rendered by the *qawwali* singers.

The fair at Jaisalmer, is a cultural and cattle fair, held for three days, in the heart of the Thar Desert in January/ February. It transforms the desert-town into a rainbow hue of colours and with magnificent folk dances and music, camel races, swirling skirts and colourful turbans. The dunes at Sam and Khuri are open-air stages for folk dancers and plays enacted by moonlight. The most charming dances of Rajasthan, the *ghair*, *dhap*, *ghoomar* and *teratali* are performed here.

The Nagaur Cattle Fair is attended solely by menfolk. It is an rustic fair with wild races and an authentic rural ambience. The Elephant Fair at Jaipur has splendid processions of the magnificent animals, decorated in full regalia, carrying *howdahs*. There are elephant polo matches, races, and other events.

Like other Indian festivals, those of Rajasthan have a religious significance. They celebrate the cycle of the seasons, spring, monsoon and the harvest. There is a blend of social tradition, worship, and festivity. These occasions are made unique by the special Rajasthani touch of flamboyant colours and vivacity. Teej, is celebrated in August, on the day Goddess Parvati was united with her husband, Lord Shiva. It also welcomes the monsoon. Women, dressed in gorgeous clothes, come out in procession, singing and praying on their way to the temples. The gardens are bush-green after the first showers, and swings are tied to branches of the trees for women and children to enjoy the cool weather. The most colourful Teej is held at Jaipur where silver and gold images of Parvati, in ceremonial palanquins, are taken out in royal processions.

Gangaur is also associated with the worship of Parvati and Shiva. Celebrations continue for a fortnight after the festival of Holi in the month of April. Drummers, musicians, and dancers follow wooden images of the deities and the most colourful procession begins with thousands of gorgeously dressed women in the lead, singing together. Women gather poppy flowers to make garlands for the goddess and in Udaipur, there are processions of boats on Pichola Lake. Tribals move in groups from village to village and young people get an opportunity to mix freely.

Holi, the exuberant festival of colours, welcomes the few precious weeks of spring and the time is for the harvest of crops. It is a joyous carnival, in which coloured powder and water is sprayed on each and everyone. On this day, there are no distinctions made, of caste or creed. The night before, a bon fire is lit to symbolically destroy evil. Holi also celebrates the sacrifice made by Holika, the sister of Hiranyakashyapu, to save Prahlad.

Dusshera is a ten-day festival celebrating the victory of Lord Rama over the wicked demon king Ravana, who abducted Rama's wife, Sita. Through the ten days the folk theatre of *Ramleela* is enacted everywhere on makeshift stages and people stay up late into the night to watch the shows. On the tenth night, huge paper and tinsel effigies of Ravana, his son Meghnadh and brother Kumbhakarna go up in a shower of fireworks. Held in October, Dusshera also heralds the second harvest season.

Diwali, arrives a fortnight after Dusshera. This was the day when Lord Rama returned to his capital city of Ayodhya and the people welcomed him with lighted oil lamps. During this magical festival of lights, as dusk falls, towns and villages turn into fairylands of glowing oil lamps as people worship the Goddess Lakshmi and Lord Ganesh. Around the Shekhawati region, the trading community of Marwaris begin their financial year on Diwali. The dark moonless sky turns silver and gold with showers of fireworks, as people greet each other with sweets and good wishes.

In Pabuji ka Phad, the *bhopas*, traditional bards, retell the exploits of Pabuji, a fourteenth-century hero. The performance goes on all night with the ballad being sung before a painted scroll that is ten metres long and two metres wide. It relates incidents from the hero's life. The *bhopa* sings, playing the stringed *ravanhatta* while his wife dances, holding up an oil lamp so that the images on the scroll coincide with the narrative.

The Jodhpur Rathores patronised the Langha musicians while the Bhattis of Jaisalmer are credited with fostering the Manghaniyar balladeers who invoke Lord Krishna with whose blessings, Jaisalmer was founded. The Pandavani balladeers who narrate the epic *Mahabharata* are also Manghaniyar singers.

With the quicksilver movements, of a dazzling classical dancer, the village women sway to the beats of the folk drummer. The mellow voice of a minstrel, praises the valour of Rajput heroes in a palace courtyard while, the plaintive cry of *maand* singers echo across sand dunes. These are some of the magical and unforgettable aspects of the music and dance of this desert land.

The performing arts, be it classical or folk, have flourished in Rajasthan blessed by the patronage of the Rajput royal houses. Rajput courts patronized music and dance in the manner of the Mughal court. In fact, it was said that a true aristocrat can be identified by his fondness for "*raag, baagh, poshak, madh, kavita aur tasvir,*" that is, by his appreciation of, music, gardens, dress, wine, poetry and painting. Painters and stone carvers had ateliers and workshops to create in stone and manuscripts bewitching fantasies at the behest of their royal patrons. Singers and dancers were maintained by the courts preserving, unchanged, age-old traditions. Jaipur, still has its own *gharana*, to teach the famous Kathak dance. Originally, it was performed by the nautch girls at the palace. Today this dance, with its intricate footwork and pirouettes, is considered one of the classical forms. The School of Jaipur, has its own special place, in the Kathak tradition.

Folk dances are an integral part of Rajasthan and can be seen at family celebrations, festivals, and fairs. Communal dances are the highlight of tribal life and the dance of the Bhils called *Ghoomar* is very popular. It is performed by women, and accompanied by the beat of drums. Women form a circle around the drummer, dancing in rhythmic pirouettes with their large skirts swirling out in waves of colour. Sometimes, dancers carry small sticks and strike them in intricate, rhythmic beats, as they weave their way in and out of the circle.

In contrast, the exuberant *gair* is an all-male performance. Dancers wear long flowing robes gathered at the waist. Each costume weighing up to thirty kilograms. The cost of these elaborate dresses is met by contributions from the community or village. The dancers move with slow measured steps in a large circle. Each dancer holds two long and thin sticks, one in each hand, which are struck alternately against the sticks held by the other dancers on either side. They often dance the *gair* to the song "*Phagun Ayo*" simulating Krishna's dance with the gopis or milkmaids.

The *Teratali* is performed at the shrine of Ramdev at Pokharan. In this intriguing dance, *manjiras*, rows of small cymbals, are tied on the body of the dancer, along the right leg, the arms and head. Dancers balance metal water pots on their head, and sometimes even hold a sword clenched in their teeth. Sitting on stage, they sway and move to the drone of the *chautara* and the beat of the *dholak*, striking the *manjiras*, creating a delightful tinkling sound. Women carry a row of earthen pitchers on their heads and sway in the graceful dance of the *panhiharin* or water carriers. This dance depicts women going to fetch water, a familiar sight in the desert, where they often travel for long hours to find clear water. The Jasnathis of Bikaner and Churu specialize in a mesmerising fire dance, where, after a dramatic build-up by drums and flutes, the dancers, step over brightly glowing embers, a feat which leaves the audience spellbound.

Kacchi ghori, the dummy-horse dance is performed on festive occasions. The torso of the dancer protrudes from the dummy horse and they wave swords in a mock battle, requiring perfect coordination among the dancers. During marriage processions, the *kacchi godi* dancers lead the procession and perform an enthusiastic battle dance with the bride's group in a show that is full of rustic charm. The Kalbelias are traditional snake-charmers.

Kachchi Ghori is an enchanting folk-dance in which the dancer wears a torso of a dummy horse. Both the dancer and the dummy horse are colourfully dressed.
Preceding page: The balladeer sings in his much practised, cultivated voice while the *sarangi* player shows his virtuosity at the stringed instrument. Manganiya, the music makers, are mostly itinerant by nature.

Their dance mimics the mesmeric movements of snakes. The female dancers always dress in black clothes, gorgeously embroidered with shimmering silver and wear bright jewellery. In the pirouetting performance of the Kalbelia, dancers bend backwards and forwards and turn in slow, sensuous swaying movements, that gather momentum until they reach an electrifying peak, to the accompaniment of drums and flutes.

As with dance, the royal houses also patronised music and employed court singers who nurtured schools of classical music. The Jaipur *gharana* is justly renowned for its *khayal* and *dhrupad* styles of classical singing. The *maand* is a typical Rajasthani form, of semi-classical music, with a milieu, a text, and a structure of its own that has a kinship with both the *thumri* and *tappa* forms, as also popular folk music. M*aand* singers, traditionally accompanied the army during military campaigns, extolling the ancestral glory of their rulers. This oral tradition has often proved to be of immense value to historical research, especially when tracing dynastic genealogies.

Today, the folk musicians remain the repositories of oral and bardic traditions. Their narratives and songs celebrate both, the gods and the glorious exploits of folk heroes and legendary lovers. The musical instruments used as accompaniment during the performances are simple ones. They are neither too sophisticated nor beyond the reach of the poor, itinerant minstrel. Among string instruments is the *sarangi* which is played with a bow, and the *ravanhatta*, a primitive instrument made with a coconut shell, a bamboo rod and two strings that produces a sonorous sound. It is the haunting strains of the *ravanhatta* that provide the background to the performance of the *bhopas*, the travelling minstrels. They also use the *jantar* that resembles the *rudra veena* with four strings, and fourteen frets. Another double-stringed instrument is the *kendru*. The four-stringed drone instrument used by musicians accompanying the *teratali* dancers is called the *chautara*. The *ghoralio* resembles a jewish harp, while the simplest and most popular instrument, carried by every itinerant singer, is the *ektara* with its single string mounted on a bamboo stick. The musicians play a variety of flutes— the *peli*, a short flute, the *algoza*, a double flute, the *satara*, a double flute of different lengths, the *naad*, a single long flute and the *surnai*. The *surnai* resembles the more popular *shehnai* of North India. The Kalbelias use the rounded *poongi*, also used by snake charmers throughout the country.

There is also a wide variety of drums. Single-faced, shallow-rimmed drums carried by folk dancers are called *daf* and *chang*. Large conical battle drums or *nagaras*, are played at the head of processions. Even everyday vessels are used to make music—a popular example is the *thali* which is a metal plate. In Jaisalmer, it is filled with water to create exotic musical notes known as *jhalar*. The *ghara*, the common earthenware pitcher, is often turned into a percussion instrument and played as an accompaniment to bells and cymbals.

The parade of bullock carts during the Teej festival celebrates the arrival of monsoon when married girls visit their parents. *Following page:* Gair, at the Jaisalmer desert fair. The all male folk-dance requires great verve and energy. The music, chiefly the beat of the drum, infuses rhythmic movements and gusto.

Wrestling is an immensely popular sport, in the villages—the fair at Banethi, provides a grand display of this ancient sport, witnessed by a magnificent crowd.

Preceding page: Ghoomar is a popular dance with the women, dressed in splendid colours and glorious jewellery, moving in a circle of sheer enchantment to the accompaniment of drum beats.

Ludnooth—or how many of you can clamber onto a solitary camel's back? This wonderful, rustic sport, requires perfect ploy, fitness, and sheer grit, to attempt a fifth, sixth, or seventh try to join other participant on the back of the camel.

At the Pushkar fair huge crowds descend to the Jyestha Pushkar lake and have their ritual dip on the Kartik Poornima.
Following page: The giant ferris wheels at the Pushkar fair beckon hundreds of men, women, and children — all awaiting their turn, to go up, amidst shouts of excitement.

Muslims offer Id prayers in front of the Hawa Mahal in Jaipur.

Page 124-125: In glittering long *jamas* and gorgeous turbans, male folk-dancers prepare for a spectacular performance at the Desert Fair in Jaisalmer.

महिला द्वार

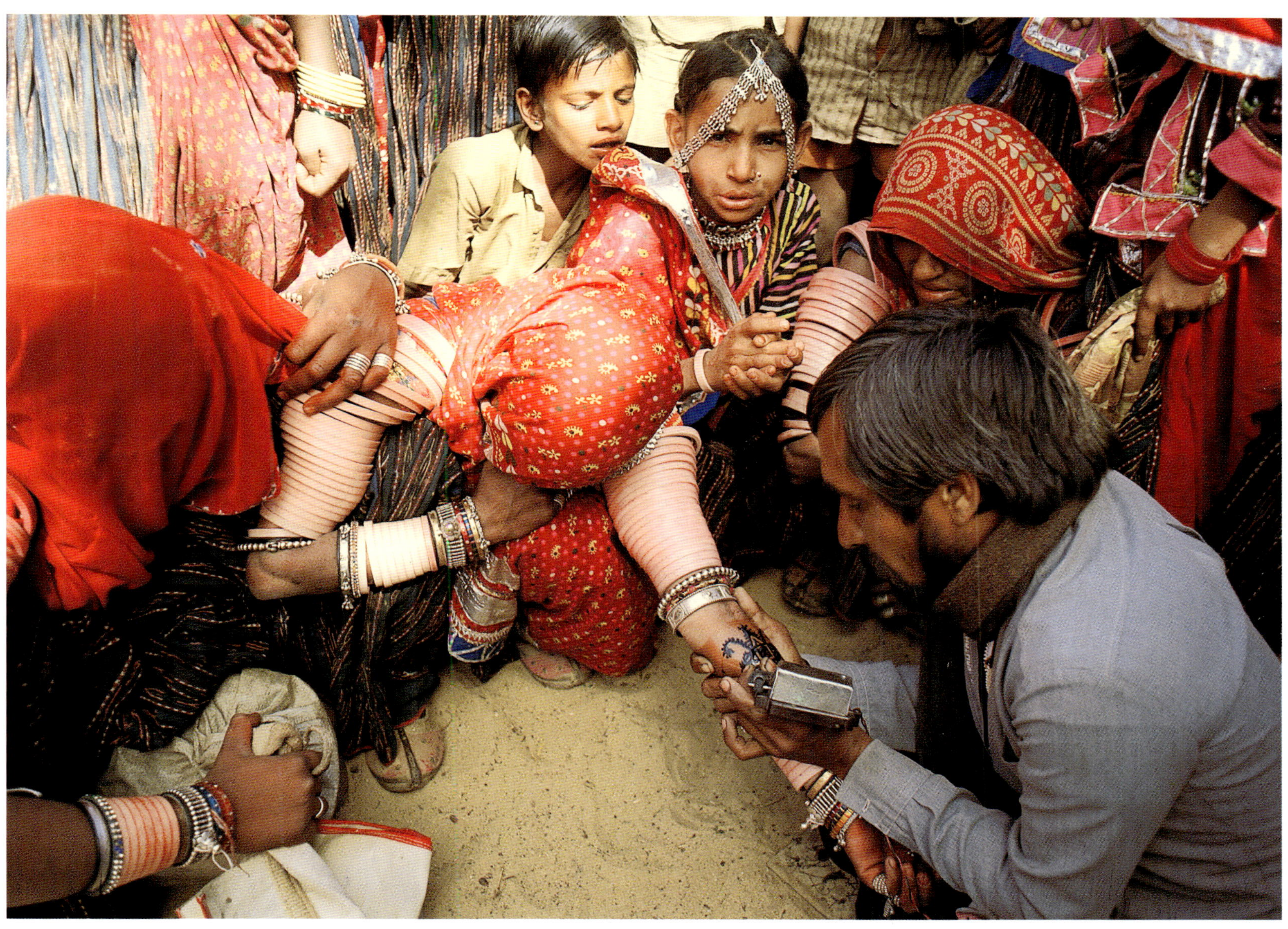

The tattoo artist does good business—as, women in particular, have their hands tattooed.

Opposite page: Village fairs in Rajasthan witness feverish activity, there are bargains to be had, visits to temples, and a variety of entertainment. Tired menfolk relax under the sun while women exchange gossip.

Following page: Pushkar Camel fair is the greatest event in the cultural diary of Rajasthan. It is a riot of colour, music, and dance besides the all important business of trade in camels.

Page130-131: The Chaksu fair in Jaipur is another grand affair when thousand of men and women come for both entertainment and business. Such occasion are not frequent and the village women are particularly keen to visit such fairs.

Temples of Rajasthan

The ceiling of the Vimala Vasahi temple in Mt. Abu
is an unparalleled splendour of white marble — it draws hundreds of visitors to the precincts everyday.
Preceding page: The Chaumukha temple in Ranakpur, dedicated to Adinatha, the first Tirthankara,
was built in the 15th century — it contains 1444 marble pillars, each one of which is differently carved.

Life for the Rajputs, came as a blessing from their gods. Before they rode out to wage a battle, they first invoked the gods and thanked them for their bounty and prayed for the blessings of their favourite deity. In happier times, they celebrated their festivals with colourful vivacity. Every Rajput clan has, a family deity, that they worship with great faith and fervour. And, when they began the building of a fort, a temple to the "clan deity" was usually the first to be built.

The *Vaastu Shastra*, an ancient treatise on the art of building, laid down the basic principles of design for all Hindu temples. In Rajasthan, temples have elaborate gateways and carved outer walls, but the *sanctum* - sanctorum is always a Spartan chamber. It is surrounded by a circumambulating path, and topped by a vertical or curvilinear spire. Additional halls, often attached to the *sanctum*, are used for ritual offerings and for feeding the poor. Among these are, the *ranga-mandapa* or assembly hall, *the bhoga-mandapa*, where devotees make offerings to the deity, and the *nata-mandapa*, where dance and music performances were held.

Most temples have a tank, or are located near a waterbody such as a river or lake. Many larger complexes have within a walled courtyard, minor shrines that are installed with supporting deities. The exterior of the temple is fabulously ornamental, and covered with figurative, geometric, and floral carvings. Tableaux of hunting celebrations and images of royalty are also frequently seen. These temples are the finest examples of the art of the *shilavat* or stone-carvers of Rajasthan. They were mostly built in clusters in remote areas, away from the path of invaders and plunderers. But they draw, even today, an endless stream of devotees. Ancient trade routes, to the ports of Gujarat and the Middle East passed through the Thar Desert. Both traders and invaders were familiar with the topography of this sector. The Aravalli range in Mewar, provided a natural defence to the temples that were mostly built on hill tops and within densely forested areas. The Jains, chose very secluded spots to build their temples, this helped to foster meditation and encourage the spirit of renunciation. Vaishnava and Shaivite temples were popular congregational centres for the devotees, whose day began with a ritualistic visit to the shrines. Age-old traditions of pilgrimage, to holy places, kept alive the light of faith in these abodes of the gods. Shrines in the sand engulfed tracts of Marwar and beyond are still difficult to visit, but inaccessibility helped to save these temples from plunder by Islamic forces in medieval times. Their inaccessibility, contributes, to their present charm and grandeur.

The superbly carved, twin Vasahi temples at Dilwara in Mount Abu, are located in the verdant hills. These Jain temples are small, but the profusion of delicate carvings on every inch of available surface, makes each of them gems. Vimal Vasahi was dedicated to the first Jain Tirthankara, Adinatha, by Vimal Sah, a minister in the Solanki court. Built on a sacred spot where Vimal unearthed the black stone image of Adinatha or Rishabhadev as he is known, the temple has fifty-two cells around the courtyard with sculpted figures within each niche. The most beautiful creations are the "*makara torana*" or scroll arches that curve over the gateways like stone garlands. Every marble pillar and ceiling has been beautifully carved and no two pillars are alike. Particularly remarkable are sixteen bracket figures of the goddesses of learning, each contained within a carved aureole. It is, however, the apex of the ceiling which is the crowning glory of sculptural art, "a dream-like vision, looming in the half light, like some marvellous underwater formation in coral and mother of pearl." Luna Vasahi, is dedicated to the twenty-second Tirthankaras of the Jains, Neminatha, and has an equally grand ceiling in the *ranga-mandapa*. The overhanging lotus, carved out of a single block of marble, is a miracle of craftsmanship as its petals have been chiselled to effect amazing detail. There are exquisite bass reliefs and images of donors along the walls.

The Achaleshwar Mahadev Temple at Achalgarh is not famous for its architectural splendour but because, it is an ancient shrine and an important place of pilgrimage. The temple was built during the reign of Rana Kumbha. There is no traditional Shiva Lingam in the *sanctum*, but, only a pit with a toe-shaped rock. Legend says Lord Shiva lost a toe here while trying to steady the wobbling Mount Abu. Shiva's vehicle, Nandi made in brass, faces the spot where the *linga* would have been enshrined.

The temples at Ranakpur are surrounded by picturesque hills and stand by the River Maghai. The land, in a secluded valley in the Aravalli Hills, was donated by the Rana to the Jains to build the temples. The renowned Chaturmukha temple dedicated to Adinatha rises on a high plinth. Several towers, rising from the walls create a rugged and formidable camouflage for the sculptural splendours contained within. The central Chaturmukha temple, is a four-faced structure dedicated to Adinatha and is a maze of twenty-nine halls. It is cruciform in plan, with four identical entrances. The interior is an ingenious distribution of space between open and covered areas with pillared halls providing the stage for the dramatic chiaroscuro effect. The sanctum stands at the centre of the large court and contains four metres high images of the first Tirthankara Adinatha. The interior comprises of a bewildering forest of pillars, believed to be 1444 in number and each one, differently carved. The entrance remains the most decorative element of the interior and the ceilings are breathtakingly beautiful. Some individual panels are visually stunning, particularly the panel depicting the legend of Parsvanatha, standing in meditation, under the protective thousand hoods of the serpent he had once rescued from a fire. A small Surya temple at Ranakpur is also ascribed to Rana Kumbha and contains exquisite sculptural ornamentation. The most beautiful are the friezes depicting the various forms of Surya, the sun god, shown riding his seven-wheeled chariot across the sky.

The town of Nagda, has some ancient rock edicts, inscriptions, and pre-historic shrines. Most of the important shrines, built over the Baghela Lake, have collapsed except the Sas Bahu temple complex called "the mother-in-law and daughter-in-law temples." They were built on a high plinth and are

This image of the twenty-third Jain Tirthankara, Parsvanatha, in the Chaumukha Temple at Ranakpur depicts him protected by snakehoods. On top are two elephants lustrating Parsvanatha by sprinkling water over him.

approached through a magnificent gateway. The smaller, known as the Bahu temple, has splendid pillars and the ornamental ceiling has eight female figures on brackets, sadly, the whole interior has been savagely mutilated and burnt. The Sas temple, bigger and more elaborate in structure, has some grand sculptural decorations on the porch, entrances, latticed windows and a magnificent ceiling raised on richly carved, cusped arches. Noted historian James Fergusson ranks the Sas temple, "among the most beautiful in the region."

The Eklingji temple, a famous complex of nearly 108 temples contains a four-faced *mukhalinga* of Shiva sculpted in black marble. Architecturally, the temple is a magnificent creation with a pyramidal roof over the *mandapa*. The pillared porch is decorated with hundreds of circular knobs. Eklingji, is the family deity, of the Mewar rulers and the royal investiture of the Sisodias takes place at the shrine. Bappa Rawal, founder of the Guhilot dynasty, spent his childhood here at the hermitage of Harit *rishi* who later invested his pupil with the royal insignia and title of "Diwan of Eklingji," which has been held by all subsequent rulers of the dynasty.

Nathdwara is the most important pilgrimage centre of the Vallabhacharya sect. The *haveli*, houses the image of Krishna as Srinathji. The image was removed from Govardhan near Mathura during the reign of Aurangzeb. Fearing religious persecution, the Vallabhacharya sect asked for the help of the Mewar ruler, Raj Singh I. Legends relate, that when the image was being transported on a chariot the wheels sank in the mud at this site signifying the god's desire to reside at that very spot. So Raj Singh I had the image installed at the *haveli* by the River Banas and it is now known as Nathdwara or Home of the Lord. Nathdwara is famous for its gorgeous *picchwais*—paintings on cloth that are hung behind the deity. The idol is carved in black marble and decorated with the costliest or jewels and diamonds. Dwarkadish ranks high among pilgrimages of the Vaishnavite sects. It is a seventeenth-century *haveli* located near Lake Rajsamund. In nearby Kankroli, can be found one of the largest inscriptions in Sanskrit. Here, more than one thousand Sanskrit verses were carved on twenty-seven stone slabs.

The Jagdish temple at Udaipur, built by Jagat Singh stands on a high terrace. It is a fine specimen of temple architecture of the period. A bronze Garuda, the mythical bird the *vahana* of Lord Vishnu sits in a pavilion facing the *sanctum*. Close to the City Palace, the Jagdish Temple overlooks the Pichhola Lake.

The most formidable fort in Mewar, Chittorgarh, contains some splendid temples that are still fairly well preserved. The Samideshwar, covered with abundant

The tortoise in silver, at the Brahma Temple in Pushkar, functions as a receptacle for the offerings made by the devotees.

sculptural decoration, is built near Gomukh, the sacred pool which is a source of permanent water supply to the rocky plateau. The Kumbha Shyam temple, is dedicated to Lord Vishnu in his incarnation as the boar, the Varaha Avatara. The spire soars elegantly to the sky and a smaller temple, popularly attributed to Mirabai, the sixteenth century saint and poetess of Mewar, stands within the precincts of the Kumbha Shyam. The Kalika temple, on the eastern rampart, is a much rebuilt structure, originally dedicated in the ninth century to Surya, the sun god. The Adbhut Mahadev temple, is a small gem of temple architecture. The Mahavirswamy Jain temple originally called the temple of Chandraprabhu another Tirthankara, stands close to the Kirti Stambha, forming a compact structural group.

The rugged, hilly terrain around Kota and Bundi has a few splendid temples, that are not frequented by visitors to this magnificent region. Menal was once the cultural centre of the Hada Rajputs. Situated near a deep gorge, it was a famous Shaivite centre and Menal or *mahanal* means the great gorge. Prithviraja Chauhan built the grand Mahaleshvara Temple on the river Menal. Rocks, boulders, gushing torrents, huge trees and a great gorge provide a background of undisturbed wilderness. The noble edifice stands within a stately courtyard and both the *sanctum* and the porch are topped by spires in a unique design that has miniature replicas clinging to the main spire. The domed ceiling of the porch has sculpted, concentric circles rising over majestic columns joined by beams. The whole interior, is covered with lavish sculptural decorations. The *sanctum* contains a *lingam* installed in a pit filled with water. Only three out of the nearly one hundred temples originally built at Bijolia, survive today. In the tenth century it was a great cultural centre of the Chauhans. Though in ruins, these Shiva temples are still magnificent structures. They stand over a water reservoir with stepped stone embankments, covered with inscriptions of tremendous historical value. The complete genealogy of the Chauhan dynasty and an early mention of the city of Dhilli (Delhi) dated 1170, is inscribed at the site. The Menal and Bijolia temples are of the Bhumija style—and one remarkable, for the intricacy of their carvings, elaborate ornamentation and unique style of the *shikharas* or towers. The *shikhara* is divided by four bands, called *latas* as they rise vertically from the four cardinal points. The spaces between the *latas* are covered with replicas of the *shikhara*. The replicas decrease in size as they converge towards the neck of the main spire.

The secluded Baroli complex, south-west of Kota, contains in the midst of a picturesque forest a ninth century Shiva shrine, the Ghateshwar temple. The porch, ceilings and pillars carry rich sculptural decorations, particularly of Shiva in his

various manifestation or *vuhas*. The entrance to the porch is a sculptural masterpiece and the independent structure of the assembly hall added after a century is an elegant creation. There is a charming image of Vishnu, resting or *syana* on the giant serpent Ananta, in one of the small shrines by the tank.

The town of Pushkar, is unique, as it has the only important shrine to Brahma, the Lord of Creation. Legend has it that Lord Brahma killed a demon here with a lotus and where the petals fell appeared, three lakes. Then, Brahma, decided to perform a *yagna* or fire sacrifice, however, his consort, Goddess Saraswati was late in arriving for the rituals. So, Brahma, married a local *Gujjar* girl named Gayatri, who performed the rituals with him. A furious Saraswati cursed Brahma that he would be forgotten by his devotees and only worshipped at Pushkar. The town also holds an annual fair for twelve days in the Hindu month of Kartik or November and it is one of the largest camel fairs in the world. For pilgrims, a bath in the lake is essential and the shores of the lake are lined by fifty-two bathing *ghats*, with flights of stone steps.

Any account of Rajasthan must include temples within the fortress of Amber. The site has been a Shaivite pilgrimage centre since ancient times as Amber is a version of Ambikeshvara, a name of Lord Shiva. Once the Kachhwahas shifted their capital to Jaipur, Amber was deserted and the temples fell into decay. People still worship at the Jagat Shiromani temple, an architectural masterpiece having a magnificent arched entrance guarded by two majestic elephants in white marble. The image of Garuda, Lord Vishnu's vehicle stands outside. The Kali temple, dedicated to Shitla Mata is the family shrine of the Kacchwahas. When Man Singh I was the Mughal Governor in Bengal, he brought the idol from Jessore. The doorway is framed by two banana plants carved out of green marble and the shrine has a solid silver door. The royal family of Jaipur still worships here.

The Karni Mata temple at Deshnok, south of Bikaner, is a much-venerated shrine. Rao Bika, a Jodhpur prince, the founder of Bikaner State, was accosted at Deshnok village by a miracle-working goddess, regarded as an incarnation of Durga. He was blessed by her with success in his mission, and in due course, Bika carved out a kingdom for himself in the desert. Karni Mata came to be worshipped as the titular deity of the Bikaner rulers. Behind exquisitely carved silver doors stands a vermilion covered idol of the goddess on a small pedestal in the sanctuary. What makes this temple so unusual is that it houses an enormous population of rats. Devotees take care, not to harm the rodents as they are believed to be the souls of *charanas*, a caste of bards awaiting rebirth.

The Brahma Temple, Pushkar has an incessant stream of visitors who, after taking a dip in the sacred lake, pay homage to Lord Brahma, the Creator of the Universe. This is the only temple in India, dedicated to Lord Brahma.

श्री जगतपिता ब्रह्मा जी का मन्दिर पुष्कर

Every inch of surface, in the interiors of the temple, receives utmost attention when the painters' brush, recreates scenes of Rajasthani culture, battles, and royalty.

Preceding page: The Nathdwara temple, dedicated to Lord Krishna, is visited by hundreds of devout men and women. Here a procession of bulls, passes through the narrow temple street.

Visitors await their turn, to pay obeisance to the magnificent Krishna image in the Nathdwara temple which opens to visitors at selected hours only.

The small ceiling at Ranakpur, creates a small riddle—five human bodies with only one head, an example of clever artistry.
Opposite page: The Surya temple at Ranakpur is profusely decorated with sculptures on the exterior.
Following page: The silver doors with a repousse image of the goddess flanked by the sacred rats at the Karni Mata temple in Bikaner. The visitor feels blessed if touched by the sacred rats which are scampering in large numbers within the temple precincts.

Handicrafts

Elephants, symbols of royal pomp and splendour, symbolize the warrior spirit of the Rajputs — they are depicted as decorative motifs on walls *(preceding page)* and in various other art forms.

The jeweller, bent over a fragile silver and turquoise enamelled earring, and the potter moulding a handful of clay into an elegant long-necked vase are but only two examples of the many talented craftsmen of Rajasthan. No other state can match the style and originality of the crafts of this desert.

The desert, has a merciless summer, with endless days of searing heat and swirling dust storms. In winter, a cruel, chilly wind blows through the night and often well into the day. Living as they often do, in far-flung hamlets, the desert dwellers accept their isolated situation—cut off from urban life by endless tracts of sandy and inhospitable terrain. Their rhythm of life, is determined by the seasons—which allows the people long stretches of time during which they create the most beautiful of handicrafts. As if in defiance of the monochromatic landscape and the many rigours of survival, their creations are vivid, colourful, and exuberant—they are fashioned with a care bordering on worship. Even objects, as functional as the simple water pot, or a pair of leather shoes, are ornamented and imbued with a beauty not usually associated with articles of daily use. Travellers, wandering from village to village will be amazed at the ways in which art and utility are combined to define the magical aesthetics of rural Rajasthan. Even exteriors of small village huts are decorated with textured patterns or drawings—of flowers and vines, images of goddess Laxmi, as well as horses and elephants. The mud walls are also patterned with simple geometrical lines and dots that are woven into intricate designs patterns made with a mixture of red sand and white lime. Women wear clothes, embellished with mirrors and embroidery, while the men tie turbans that flare out, in the most vibrant of colours. They even decorate their camels, snipping their fur into imaginative patterns, studding the saddles with sequins and brass and creating lively trappings with beads and bells, weaves and patch work.

The metal art of Rajasthan dates back to 300 BCE. This is testified by the discovery of copper beads, bangles, and tools during the excavations at Kalibangan. The artefacts unearthed reveal, that artisans created objects of both utility and beauty. Copper was a much favoured metal and used to make tools. The bronzes found at Vasantgarh, near Mt. Abu, suggest a high level of craftsmanship as early as the seventh century CE. Over the centuries, metallurgical skills and innovations evolved, to often produce exquisite objects. Rural Rajasthani women, wear heavy jewellery made of silver and ivory. This chunky, carved, silver jewellery has now caught the eye of the sophisticated, urban woman who wears it as a symbol of ethnic chic. The richer urban classes, prefer jewellery made of precious stones and gold, designed and crafted into elegant masterpieces. Jaipur has become the largest emerald cutting centre in the world, and is renowned for its delicate enamelled jewellery. The Aravallis have bestowed the state with rich deposits of precious and semi-precious stones. Rubies, garnets, amethyst, topaz, lapis-lazuli and jade are also cut in Jaipur by craftsmen whose skills have been honed through generations.

Gem-cutters and polishers have perfected the art of cutting and faceting, acquiring a high degree of expertise. They can be seen, in their workshops, in Jaipur's Johari Bazaar, using tools which have remained unchanged through the centuries.

Ornamental enamelled jewellery, called *minakari*, is the legacy of five skilled enamel artists. They were invited, in the sixteenth century from Lahore by Raja Man Singh I to settle down in Amber. They helped to create, this stunning method of ornamentation. The engraving is a painstaking and highly skilled craft. The surface depressions are serrated with a steel stylus so as to secure the enamel and to augment the play of light and shade. Colours with the highest resistance to heat are set first and red, is always set at the end. Firing in the kiln requires fine-tuned and precision timing. Finally, the jewellery is cleaned with a tamarind solution and polished with corundum to bring out the lustrous hues. *Kundan* work is a more costly, gorgeous version of gold enamel work. Precious stones are studded into gold on one side in different patterns and the reverse is ornamented with coloured enamel. Floral patterns, being the most favoured. Jaipur, is also a renowned centre for enamelling on brass and silver trinkets, vases, bowls, boxes, plates and many other gift items. Hand-beaten brass, is first serrated with an overall pattern, and carefully applied enamel highlights the delicate tracery. Tradition has provided poetic names for these designs. *Chikan*, is a bold floral ornamentation set off by chased and lacquered surfaces, while *marori*, is a fine lacquered pattern covering the entire surface, and, in *bichi*, floral and leaf motifs are spread out over a chased and lacquered background.

During the heydays of the *maharajas*, damascening or the encrusting of gold and silver wires to metal surfaces was in great demand. This form of ornamentation was used for personal weapons, swords, hilts, scabbards, daggers and shields. Intricate designs were created with Quranic verses and inscriptions in different calligraphic scripts as well as floral motifs and geometrical arabesques. Today, this ancient craft survives only in Jaipur and Alwar. At Pratapgarh, near Chittorgarh, craftsmen produce a very different style of metalware called *thewa*. Geometric and floral arabesques, battle and hunting scenes, and religious images are all cut out on thin gold sheets and the silhouetted relief is mounted and fused on to glass. The process is completed with fixing of a thin silver foil on the back of the glass to obtain a uniform lustre. The *thewa* artists produce the most charming jewellery boxes, perfume bottles, and vases.

Among the rich variety of textiles for which Rajasthan is renowned, is the *bandhani*, the art of tie and dye fabrics, that has been perfected in ancient times. The stunning effect of contrasting colour combinations make the *bandhani* fabric the most coveted part of a bride's trousseau. The pattern of dots and squares is obtained by a fine knotting technique, executed with dexterity and expertise. It is possible to manipulate this quaint method, with a virtually limitless variety of designs. The fabric is dipped into a dye. The knotted parts do not absorb the dye; and, when the knots are opened the pattern stands revealed. Jodhpur and Udaipur are justly renowned for the stunning variety of their splendid *bandhani* fabrics. Udaipur, produces the *lehariya*, an elegant wavy pattern, the multi-coloured stripes of which are called *chira*. The *ekladi* fabrics, on the other hand have a pattern of small circles and squares. The *tikhunti*, *chaukhunti*, *charbandi* and *satbandi* are progressively more complicated variations of the dots. Human and animal figures are formed in *shikari* patterns. Reds, oranges, and yellows are the most cherished colours, since they are regarded as being very auspicious.

Once upon a time, the fabled block-printed textiles of Rajasthan travelled to the Middle East and Europe by the Silk Route. Treasured by connoisseurs, their splendid designs have survived the centuries. Sanganer and Bagru, both are famous for this craft and are mostly inhabited by *cheepas*, a hereditary caste of hand-block printers. The traditional Sanganer print is made on pale yellow or light brown cotton, worked with classic floral motifs. The wooden blocks used for printing are finely carved with floral, geometric, and animal motifs and preserved as art objects. These blocks, lift the required colour from dye-soaked pads and are then pounded swiftly onto lengths of fabric with a remarkable coordination of the eyes and the hands. It is an amazing sight to watch the craftsmen print the cloth. Sanganer,

Gold (inlay) on objects made of marble indicate the craftsmen's artistry.
Following page: Exquisitely crafted wooden screens are further embellished with miniature paintings depicting Radha and Krishna as well as court scenes.

a medieval town on the banks of the River Amani Shah, was renowned, as the capital of calico printing. When its prints were exported to England, in the nineteenth century, the local textile manufacturers felt threatened and the British government did its best to control the export. Laila Tyabji makes an interesting observation about the charming chintz prints: "Incongruous, though it may seem, Jane Austen's gently nurtured heroines' sprigged—muslin were, almost certainly, block printed in Sanganer by some fiery, crimson-turbaned and ear-ringed Rajput male—his views, on the role of women, perhaps not all that different from theirs." Bagru cottons, are also block printed, using vegetable and mineral dyes and the art is a closely kept secret of the Bagru *cheepas*. Legend has it that it, was revealed to their ancestors by Surasen, the son of Arjuna, the hero of the epic *Mahabharata*. Surasen, was in ruin granted the know how, from a divine source to help him to earn his livelihood, when he was obliged to renounce his warrior class in punishment for a misdeed. The Bagru cottons are, usually, in darker hues of brick-red and black, with a linear and zig zag stripes. With increasing worldwide awareness about the need for nature-friendly products, their demand has grown. This grand revival has enabled the preservation of a once slowly-vanishing art. A variation to the Bagru block prints, is an innovative overprinting in gold and silver called *khari*. The effect produced is a shimmery fabric that is beautiful.

Barmer, specialises in geometric patterns, block-printed on blue and red cloth known as *ajrak*. The harsh desert sun and blistering heat in this sandy town, undoubtedly dictate the choice of such vibrant colours. To add a touch of dazzle, the Barmer women, embroider the fabric with tiny pieces of mirror, satin stitch motifs of dancing figures, peacocks, flowers and the circular religious motif of the *mandala*. The finest and most ethereal cotton weaves come from Kota, famed as it also, for its many other equally renowned crafts. Cotton *doria* sarees, woven with

alternating cotton and silk wefts have a subtle, ever - so delicate motif. Woven in muted shades and self-checks, the sarees are soft, lighter than air and much preferred by Indian women as elegant summer wear.

While the Rajasthani women are clad in gorgeously colourful costumes, the men, prefer stark white for both their *dhoti* and shirt. The simplicity of the male attire, so strikingly wanting in colour, is balanced by the eyecatching hues of the *pugree* or turban. Even today, when western dress is regrettably becoming common, the turban, remains an essential part of a Rajasthani male's attire. No true Rajasthani stirs out of his house without his turban and it remains a symbol of his dignity, and honour. It is truly said that in Rajasthan, women's skirts as also styles of turbans change every twenty-four miles. There is a vibrant and varied range of colours which are worn, according to the season and occasion. Bright yellow, mustard, and red are the colours of traditional celebrations and festivals. Dark blue, maroon, khaki and white denote more solemn occasions. The many different ways of tying a turban, is an art form in itself—most royal families engage men who are specialists in it. The connoisseur can guess the region a man comes from, his social status, and even his profession from the way he has tied his *pugree*. The various kinds of turbans, *pugree*, *safa* and *paag*, are tied differently. *Paag* is an immense eighteen-metre-length of cloth first twisted like a rope then wound tightly around the head. The *safa* is tied more loosely, leaving one end to hang over the back.

Textile workers produce a wide array of dhurries—woven cotton floor coverings—and splendid hand-knotted carpets in Mughal designs. Carpets woven by prisoners at the Bikaner Jail are known for their excellent designs and intricate knotting. For chilly desert nights, there are sturdy woollen blankets, like the *pattu*, woven in warm, striking colours that can be easily cut and stitched to make garments. Menfolk of Rajasthan are very partial to the sturdy embroidered *juthis*. These leather shoes with proudly curving tips, are decorated with a cheerful tassel. In the beginning, the *juthis* are hard on the feet, but quickly soften to a very comfortable footwear that is, ideal for the harsh desert. Leatherwork is a hereditary craft in Rajasthan. Men do the tanning, dyeing and stitching and then women embroider the leather with tassels, sequins, and brass studs. They make shoes, sandals, saddles, musical instruments and even water containers. Camel hide is used with great artistry, scraped to a tissueless translucence and fashioned into exquisite gift articles like water bags, pouches, and purses.

The *kumbhar*, or hereditary potter, is found in every village, making jars—to store grain and water, cooking pots, bowls, and plates. These rural craftsmen also enhance their skill to an art, embellishing the objects with beautifully decorated designs. Terracotta plaques from Molela, near Udaipur, are an unusual variation of the art. They show anthropomorphic forms of deities, snakes, and legendary folk heroes. Deities like Durga, Shiva, and Bhairon are shown on the Molela relief plaques which have a square base and triangular top. Occasionally, these images are coloured with vermilion, yellow, green, red and white but traditionally, the plaques are in the original terracotta colour. They make an eyecatching narrative series, which together, mounted on the wall create a most unusual effect. The craft of making blue-glazed pottery originated in Persia and China and was fashionable during the Mughal period. Sawai Ram Singh encouraged this craft by teaching the technique at the school of art founded by him in the nineteenth century. The pottery is not made with clay but with ground quartz stone. Wall plates, jugs, vases and ashtrays are made at Sanganer where hand painting in conventional floral and geometrical arabesques has achieved a high standard. Originally, the colours were limited to turquoise and emerald but, now, new combinations of canary yellow, dark blue, and brown have been adopted. A paper thin variety of blue pottery called *kagzi* is also made in Alwar.

The finest examples of the stone carvers' art can be seen decorating both palaces and, *havelis*, the mansions of aristocrats. Every fortress, palace, and temple has masterly examples of sculptural art—from courtyards in the Mehrangarh Fort in Jodhpur to the ceilings of the Dilwara and Ranakpur temples. Here, using hard sandstone and marble the carvers worked with the fine precision of jewellers. The facades, balconies, and windows of the *havelis* are chiselled with amazing intricacy this, finally acquiring the consistency of lace. Every centimetre of the facades are covered with the delicate filigree designs. The *havelis* at Jaisalmer, where sunlight glows on the pale gold of sandstone and flows through the lattice screens in a shimmering play of light and shadow, are particularly beautiful.

Wooden puppets, are the most heart-warming among the simple creations of the Rajasthani carpenter. These *kathputlis* as they are known, are tiny, colourfully-clad figures, with lively faces, hugely exaggerated eyes, prominent, sharp noses and very clearly outlined sensuous lips. Performing on makeshift stages in village-courtyards, halls of *havelis*, and city gardens, the male puppets, with fierce moustaches brandish their swords, ride the horses, and swagger into battle, to win the hand of the bashful maidens. They then celebrate their victory with wild dancing. Behind the backdrop, the puppeteers, the *kathputliwala*, deftly manouvers the strings as his wife sings the tales of love-lorn maidens and valiant heroes.

In Rajasthan, wood is inlaid with copper, silver wire, and bone to create chairs, table-tops and boxes. Furniture, screens, doors and caskets are also painted in motifs reminiscent of miniature paintings. Small wooden items are coloured and lacquered to make lamps, toys, and images of deities and wood is also inlaid with metal plating. Wood carvers constructed amazingly massive portals, the entrances to fortresses and palaces. These mammoth doors, studded with metal spikes and iron nails, brass and ivory have withstood several centuries of use. The gigantic teak doors from Chittorgarh were carried away to Agra by Akbar as war booty. The finest doors can be seen at the City Palace in Jaipur—some have elaborately worked brass panels, while others are framed by gorgeous frescoes which are masterpieces of craftsmanship the likes of which are not to be seen anywhere.

The designs of ethnic jewellery are inspired by traditional styles which have been in use since ancient times.
Following page: Blue pottery, brought to India from Persia during the Mughal rule, in the sixteenth century, was introduced into the repertoire of Rajasthani crafts by Raja Man Singh I (1550-1614).

Elephants, horses, and water bottles are decorated with gesso work in gold.
Opposite page: Mojris, light-weight leather shoes are a much sought after hand-crafted item from Rajasthan.
The farmers prefer unembroidered *jootis* while the richer people go in for the lighter, embroidered footwear.
Preceding page: Most exquisite examples of silver that are made in a synthesis of traditional and new experimental designs.
Enamel jewellery is yet another example of traditional art refined with fascinating new patterns.

Kasidapani embroidery of Barmer creates enchanting patterns using mostly folk, animal, and floral motifs.
Opposite page: The puppets with wide eyes and enchanting jewellery wearing gorgeous costumes are charming examples of village craft and a source of immense entertainment to the simple village folk.
Following page: The instinct to decorate their homes is evident in its purest form in the village homes of the desert — women decorate mud walls and floors with pretty motifs.

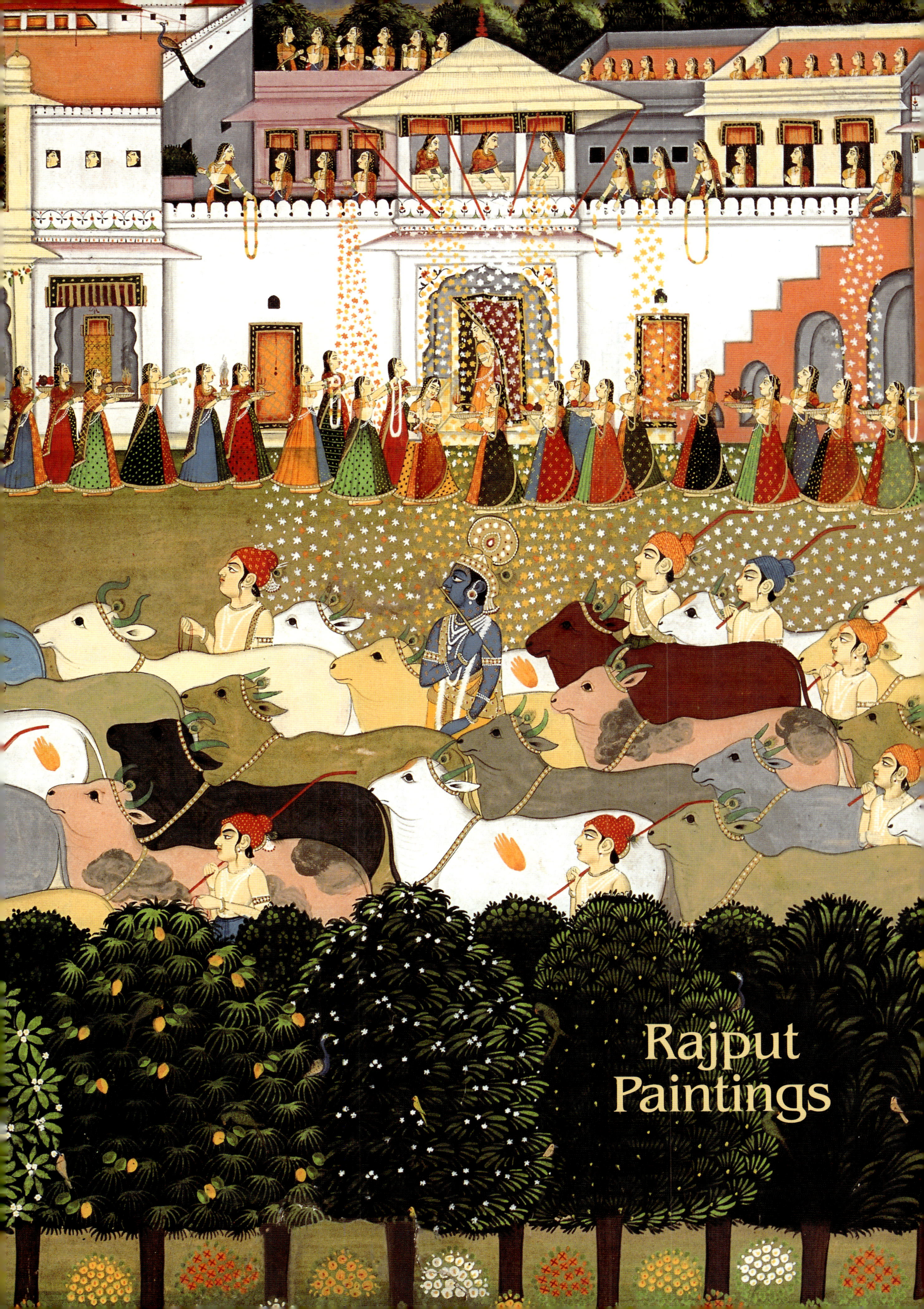
Rajput
Paintings

A hunting scene — hunting was a favourite pastime of the rulers when they were not actually engaged in battles. *Preceding page:* Krishna is the hero of the religious themes depicted in Rajasthani miniature paintings. Here Krishna is shown leading the cows back home at dusk.

It is, difficult to trace, the beginnings of Rajput painting in terms of precise dates. The tradition, stems from deep roots in the cultural history of the land. In its earliest form, painting in different regions of the country, was done on palm leaves, illustrating scriptures. These slim and delicate volumes were bound between wooden book covers and were, seldom more than two inches in width. The oldest palm-leaf paintings to survive, date to the eleventh century CE. These are the Pala-Buddhist manuscripts from Bihar and Bengal and the Jain manuscripts from Western India, comprising Gujarat, Rajasthan, and Malwa. Many palm-leaf manuscripts were destroyed during the early Muslim invasions in the twelfth century CE, but the Jains of Western India, kept these illustrated religious texts in secret *bhandaras* (libraries), some of which are still to be discovered. The *Kalpasutra*, dealing with the life of the Jain Tirthankara Mahavira, and *Kalakacharyakatha*, narrating adventures of Kalaka, a Jain monk, were the two most frequently illustrated manuscripts, both being great favourites with both patrons and painters.

Palm-leaves were gradually replaced by paper, which came from Persia in the fourteenth century CE. Blue pigment, also from Persia, replaced the solid red background used in the earlier paintings. Brushwork, from the paper period onwards, became more elaborate and the format changed from the horizontal in palm leaves to the vertical on the paper. A narrative element was introduced and there was a wider use of foliage and animal life. There was also the inclusion of elaborate architectural settings in the background of the paintings. The earliest extant Rajput paintings are the fifteenth century miniature paintings attributed to Mewar artists, though a palm-leaf manuscript is known to have been illustrated at Ahar, near Udaipur in 1260 CE. The earliest known painting on paper originates from Chittor, around 1422 CE. However, the earliest and best known group of text illustrations were possibly executed before the ultimate sack of Chittor by Akbar in 1568. These include Jai Deva's *Gita Govinda*, the *Bhagwat Purana*, and *Ragamala* paintings known as the Kuladhara group. They are so termed as the male figures are all depicted wearing small conical caps or *kulah*. The devotional character of the themes chosen for illustration was inevitable following the Hindu renaissance which spread across the whole country. The *bhakti* cult was sweeping through the whole of Northern India and the religious scriptures were now freely available to the common man and were no longer the sacred preserve of priests and temples. Vaishnavism, in particular, the Radha-Krishna theme, captured both the hearts and the minds of the people. The people of Mewar responded passionately to the poetic tradition and the mystical and erotic content of the Krishna legend.

Mewar rulers, in a subtle cultural interaction, employed Muslim artists to work in their ateliers, much the same way as Akbar recruited a large number of his painters from amongst his Hindu subjects. Mewar preserved, the quintessentially Hindu view of life as a symbol of its identity. Its painters captured the beauty of the Krishna legend, with the use of intense colour. The use of splendid architectural settings and the addition details such as pavilions and latticed marble screens indicates an awareness of the stylistic features of Mughal miniatures. There still continued, a clear emphasis on feeling and sentiment, with little regard for verisimilitude and perspective which were two distinctive features of Mughal painting.

The *Ragamala*, "the visual interpretations of Indian musical modes, previously envisioned in divine or human form by musicians and poets," was one of the cherished themes for paintings. The first *Ragamala* in Mewar was painted at Chawand in 1605 by Nisardi, a Muslim artist. This *Ragamala* served as a standard work for the next two centuries. The other *Ragamala* set was painted at Udaipur in 1628 by Sahibdin. Selected portions of the *Bhagwat Purana* and the *Ramayana* were also illustrated by Sahibdin. The *Ragamalas* and other traditional themes, form the core of conservative Rajput painting and were created within pre-set compositional models.

There was, little significant influence of Mughal painting on Mewar painting—the gardens, pavilions, *darbar* scenes, costumes and the use of finer pigments, however, reveal a superficial impact. There was no portraiture, which had turned into a distinguished genre of painting under Jahangir and certainly no experimentation in style. The Rajput artist depended heavily on poetry which presents both forms and shapes as metaphors and symbols. Faithful rendition of a theme alone sufficient and, no imaginative or creative denies was required to meet artistic obligations. Mewar painting, thus acquired a static character with no stylistic progress as was apparent in contemporary Mughal painting under Akbar, Jahangir, and Shahjahan. However, as Milo Cleveland Beach observes, it is to the credit of "the strength of the pre-Mughal traditions in Mewar that the inherent energy and vigour of the school - and of Rajput art in general - is intensified rather than diminished by greater refinement of perception and technique." Painting in Mewar continued to flourish well into the eighteenth century but without any thematic or stylistic distinction.

Painters worked in the Marwar region, throughout the fifteenth and sixteenth centuries. They followed the folk style of the Western India School of painting without any outstanding achievement. Jodhpur paintings, on the other hand acquired a distinct identity during the reign of Jaswant Singh. He was a connoisseur of the fine arts and was deeply interested in portraiture. In the early eighteenth century, Ajit Singh had the *Gita Govinda* and the *Rasikapriya* illustrated by his atelier. Hunting scenes and festivities were the other favourite subjects of Jodhpur. Elongated human figures alone betray some influence of Mughal painting. The quintessentially Rajput spirit revealed in the use of strong colours

Lord Krishna as Srinathji installed at Nathdwara, has a tremendous following all over Rajasthan. His image is portrayed in all its glory and in various forms on miniatures and on *pichhwais*, cloth paintings.

and rhythmic lines, and the domineering presence of the proud Rajput prevailed throughout the eighteenth century, long after the era of great Mughal painting. The British protection to Jodhpur encouraged Man Singh to devote himself freely to art. He commissioned paintings of texts like the *Shiva Purana*, the *Panchtantra* and *Kamasutra* as also *Ragamalas*. The use of red, yellow, green, and blue colours typically worn by desert folk is dominant and, the burly Rajputs are painted with large mutton-chop whiskers. Women wear gorgeous bell-shaped skirts and tight bodices. Man Singh appears in many of the paintings seated on a swing with his queen. Splendid architectural settings in the background contribute a touch of royal grandeur. The intensity of Jodhpur paintings gradually faded away into uninspired productions.

Bikaner painting, shows a marked Mughal influence; Ruknuddin and Nuruddin were the two most famous of Bikaner painters in the seventeenth century. They owed a great deal to their Mughal peers and incorporated new elements like space, fabric patterns, and precise and diminutive female figures. Their paintings also reveal an overall elegance and sophistication. As J.C. Harle, noted art critic and historian explains: "A dearth of local traditions arising from its isolation, may have attracted painters from Delhi after the accession of the austere Aurangzeb deprived them of patronage, for Bikaner painting reflects Mughal style and taste at various periods perhaps more than any in Rajasthan, sometimes with a richness derived from the Deccan." Deccani influence on Bikaner painting appears under Anup Singh who served Aurangzeb at Aurangabad, Bijapur, and Golconda and was rewarded for his bravery with the title of Maharaja.

The small state Kishangarh, is known for its unique and charming style of paintings which illustrated episodes from Krishna's life. Their spiritual and devotional aura emanates from the all-pervasive Vaishnava faith, the Pushti Marga, or the way of the grace of god. Elongated human figures, elegant pavilions, and a lavish use of green on panoramic landscape had already appeared in the early eighteenth century. But, it was only under Sawant Singh, that Kishangarh painting reached its zenith. Sawant was a poet and scholar of Sanskrit and Persian. He was deeply in love with a lady-in-attendance, called Bani Thani, the bewitching Lady of Fashion. This beauty of Bani Thani was used as a model of sophisticated beauty, and her face became the highly stylized facial type for the portrait of Radha—an elongated face, receding forehead, arched eyebrows, lotus-shaped eyes, a sharp nose, thin sensitive lips and a pointed chin. The divine lovers—Krishna and Radha—always appear in a land of verdant calm absorbed in each other. Many of these paintings depict the divine lovers to be idealized versions of the ruler and his beloved. Sawant Singh was particularly lucky in having Nihal Chand, an accomplished painter, in his atelier. He infused new life into his master's poetry through his

Top: This wall painting on a *haveli* depicts a royal palace, providing many clues to the architectural styles in nineteenth century Rajasthan.
Bottom: Colourful miniature paintings, depicting various aspects of life, form part of many a royal collection.

remarkable paintings. Between 1735 and 1770, Kishangarh produced a splendid set of paintings, imbued with lyricism and rare sophistication. However, within a few years of Satwant Singh's death, the Kishangarh style exhausted itself for want of that inspiration which had made its paintings so outstanding in the history of Indian art.

The two small states of Bundi and Kota were the centres of a highly innovative and inspired painting style during the seventeenth and eighteenth centuries. Haraoti, country of the Hara Rajput, was raised by the Chauhan dynasty of Ajmer. In 1625, Kota, hitherto a small segment of Bundi, was set up as an independent state and, soon, before the end of the century totally eclipsed that of Bundi. Chattar Sal of Bundi was the Governor of Delhi and campaigned for Shahjahan in the Deccan. His successor, patronized painting, but it was only under Umed Singh that Bundi paintings acquired an inspired lyrical quality and refinement. Bundi painting emerged out of the Western Indian Style to acquire a distinct identity of its own. The influence of Mewar, Mughal and Deccan styles on the work of Bundi is all too obvious but the inventiveness of the artist is never shackled by these external factors. The large, oval shape of the eyes, belongs to Mewar while the rounded female face and male costumes are Mughal. Certain facial types and the placement of architectural details are Deccani. The abundant lush greenery, nature's gift to Bundi, appears in the paintings in all its grandeur and glory—ducks frolicking in the pond, swaying plantain trees and spiked flowering plants.

A *Ragamala* painted in Chunar and dated to 1591 CE is attributed to three pupils of Mir Sayyad Ali and Abdul Samad, the earliest painters, brought from Persia by Humayun to the Mughal Court. It served as a model for many subsequent versions, and was perhaps, commissioned by Bhoj Singh who served at the Mughals at Varanasi. Pre-Mughal Bundi painting was based on conceptualising, using flat colours in large areas with a pronounced streak of sentimentality. The Mughal influence contributed an elegance to the male figures now bedecked in pearl jewellery, *jamas*, *patkas* and *churidars*, while the women are shown in *ghagharas* or *skirts* and high *cholis* or *bodices*. Shading under the armpits shows the influence of the early Mughal style. Also, instead of the full architectural setting, now only two sides of the roof are shown. Also noteworthy is, the preference for parterres and flowering bushes. A *Bhagwat Purana*, painted in 1640, was noted for its bigger format and impressive design. However, *Ragamalas* remained the favourite subject. The most distinguished feature of Bundi painting is the depiction of elephants, wild and volatile in action, hunting, and in chase. Bishan Singh was himself, fond of the big game, bivouacking for days in the open forest in pursuit of tiger. The 'White Period' (1765-1775) saw the use of an innovative technique, in the portrayal of delicate maidens at their toilette, set against a stark white background, the ivory tones

A miniature painting relating the romantic tale of Dhola of Narwar and Maruni of Poongal who were chased by the army of Umar Samra.

of the body framed within dark tresses and loose attire. These paintings have no mystical pretensions; many of them depict intimacy between lovers or women pining for their lovers. Towards the end of the eighteenth century, Bundi painting suffered a decline in quality. The technical finesse remained but inspiration had apparently deserted the painter.

Kota painting, is generally regarded, as a continuation of the Bundi style but, it overshadows the latter, in its depiction of hunting scenes, of earth-shaking confrontations between elephants, as well as its intensely detailed forest scenes. Milo Beach writes that it is for this bold adventurism that Kota painting became "the most inventive and experimental Rajput School in the seventeenth century, a position it will hold throughout much of its history." J.C. Harle also commented that in the history of Indian painting, the forest has never been painted in such natural splendour with an eye for minute detail "rendered with exceptional realism and an almost calligraphic finesse of brush strokes, extending far into the distance to broken hills with tree-lined meadows beyond and a castle."

Amber was the capital of the Kachchwaha rulers till the creation of Jaipur. It had a long tradition of mural painting. In fact, most of Amber's palaces are covered with floral designs and frescoes. Amber was the first state in Rajasthan to seek Mughal friendship when Bahar Mal married off his daughter to Akbar. Soon, Man Singh I was to rise as Akbar's most trusted general. Later, both Jai Singh I and Sawai Jai Singh II were to enjoy immense power at the Mughal court. This interaction with the Mughals had its impact on art. Work of the Kachhwaha ateliers is not much known, though floral decorations on palace walls owes its inspiration to Mughal garden pavilions and palaces. The rulers stayed in Delhi and Agra or were out on Mughal campaigns which left them with little time for finer pursuits at home.

Jaipur painting followed predictable lines of development in the absence of any active patronage. Routine paintings or familiar themes such as the *Ragamalas* and *Krishna Leela* were painted with elan. Painting under Sawai Jai Singh II rose to some prominence and a *Ragamala* series belongs to his reign in the early eighteenth century. It was under Pratap Singh that the ruler's Vaishnava faith had a direct influence on painting. Whereas, the folk element based on native traditions, was never absent the Jaipur painter was sensitive to the sophisticated palette of Mughal painting. Jaipur paintings are often large in size, and the portraits of the rulers remain the finest specimens of Hindu portraiture yet known.

Rajput folk art, is steeped in the traditions and patterns of life as was observed in villages and royal centres. In fact, states like Bundi, Kota, and Samode gave tremendous support to painters by keeping some palace interiors exclusively for artistic decoration. The Bundi *chitrashala* is virtually a grand picture gallery and Samode has magnificent murals painted in enchanting colours. Palaces at Bikaner, Jodhpur, and Jaisalmer also had frescoes covering ceilings and large parts of the walls.

The Shekhawati region has a great number of *havelis*, built mostly in the nineteenth century. The walls of the structures are covered with lively frescoes, ranging in theme from the religious to the secular. Some showing their first acquaintance with the automobile, telephone, train, aeroplane as well as of Europeans playing the gramophone or walking their dogs. *Havelis* at Sikar, Navalgarh, Mandawa, Jhunjhunu, Fatehpur, Ramgarh and Lachmangarh are veritable open-air galleries.

Rajasthani artists also deserve admiration for the equally magnificent cloth paintings made by them. *Phad* and *Pichwai* are the two forms of cloth paintings which are now amongst an art collector's most cherished possessions. *Phad* or, more precisely, Pabuji ki Phad is a large painting on coarse cotton cloth. Its theme celebrates the valour and chivalry of Pabuji, a warrior-saint of the Rathors of Jodhpur. As per the legend, Pabuji borrowed ahorsefor his marriage procession for which he pledged his help under all circumstances. Unfortunately the horse lender, a woman, required Pabuji's help against marauders who came to take away her cattle. Pabuji left his marriage ritual incomplete, fought the thieves and sacrificed his life. He kept his word of honour, and for this deed is deified and worshipped by the village folk. The itinerant *bhopas*, hereditary minstrels from Bhilwara and Chittorgarh, narrate the heroic deeds of Pabuji and other folk deities like Deonarainji and Ramdeoji, to the accompaniment of the *ravanhatta*, a stringed musical instrument. The wife of the *bhopa* joins him in this musical performance, a popular combination of folk art and music. Pabuji ki Phad, is a long painted scroll, depicting, in strong earthy colours, the chief episodes from this narrative. The artist's start work on the *phads* following devotional rituals. The process of the preparation of dyes is a closely-guarded family secret. Names of both the *bhopa* and the painter are inscribed on the *phad*. The *phad* is a sacred object, not discarded after long use but simply consigned to the waters of Pushkar lake.

Picchwai painting is, yet another form of devotional painting, executed in the traditional folk style. These large paintings on cotton, depict scenes from the life of Krishna and are used as a backdrop for the image of the deity in temples of the Pushti Marga belonging to the Vallabhacharya sect, particularly at Nathadwara near Udaipur, where Krishna is worshipped as Srinathji. Scenes like the *Raslila* depict the devotee's quest for union with the Lord symbolized in the picchwais by Krishna granting an audience to dancing milkmaids. *Picchwai* painting requires an extreme dedication to the art, and sincere devotion to Srinathji. The process of grinding stones, plants, and minerals is laborious. Families of Jangid and Adi Gaud *brahmins* in Nathadwara have preserved this sacred art for posterity. Each delicate stroke of the brush is steeped in the power and intensity of faith, and the intensity of the colours is as much a reflection of the spiritual beauty visualized by the devotee.

श्री

A painting in the Mandir Palace, Jaisalmer reflects the love Rajput rulers had to have their images painted in the typical Mughal style—riding splendid horses accompanied by a retinue of attendants. *Preceding page:* Pabuji ki Phad - a folk style of painting on long scrolls of cloth is the most representative example of folk art. Bhopas, balladeers carry it to village fairs and narrate the legend of the hero Pabuji to the accompaniment of enchanting music on the *ektara*, a stringed instrument.

Portrait of a great ruler Sawai Raja Jai Singh II, who built the city of Jaipur and Jantar Mantar — the massive buildings for astronomical studies. *Following page:* A large wall painting at Badal Mahal in Junagarh Fort, Bikaner. The portrait of a Rajput grandee sums up the legendary warrior nature of this valiant race and also its royal splendour.

सिंगार भोग
॥पद चपक॥ मिलि भोजन स्यामा
करै॥ पिय करत हित हाथ जिमा
करत विनै नैननि सौं मोहन स्र
की घरिया अटप

करतकरगसाहुसतरसवतिया
नोहूंफलपाऊंदेहधरै॥टेक॥
धाकरपरसिडरै॥श्रीभटनेह
नसैनसौंपैयावरै॥४॥

The instinct to decorate is inborn. Even the hind legs of an elephant are painted in fascinating colours to make the mighty pachyderm look enchanting. *Preceding page:* Radha and Krishna are portrayed in various moods and situations, here together in a grove attended by *gopis* - the cowherd maidens.